Tutoring and Demonstrating:
A Handbook

Editors: Fred Forster, Dai Hounsell and Sheila Thompson

Centre for Teaching, Learning and Assessment
The University of Edinburgh

in association with the

Universities' and Colleges' Staff Development Agency

Published by the

Centre for Teaching, Learning and Assessment
The University of Edinburgh
34 Buccleuch Place
Edinburgh EH8 9JS

Tel: 0131 650 4131
Fax: 0131 650 6956
Email: TLA@ed.ac.uk

in association with the

Universities' and Colleges' Staff Development Agency
Level Six
University House
Sheffield S10 2TN

Tel: 0114 282 4211
Fax: 0114 272 8705
Email: ucosda@sheffield.ac.uk

UCoSDA is an Agency of the Committee of Vice-Chancellors and Principals
of the Universities of the United Kingdom

Orders for single and discounted bulk copies should be addressed to UCoSDA

ISBN: 0 9523956 1 4

Contents

Acknowledgements and Contributors

Preparation of the material in this handbook was made possible through financial support from the Scottish Higher Education Funding Council, and their generous assistance is gratefully acknowledged.

We would like to express our thanks not only to the contributors to this handbook but also to the many other colleagues, both at Edinburgh and elsewhere, who offered advice and support and made constructive comments on earlier drafts.

Authors

Dr Iain Allison	Senior Lecturer, Department of Geology and Geophysics, The University of Glasgow
Mr Charles Anderson	Lecturer, Department of Education, The University of Edinburgh
Dr Derek Arthur	Director, Mathematical Teaching Organisation, The University of Edinburgh
Dr Kate Day	Research and Development Officer, TLA Centre, The University of Edinburgh
Dr Frances Dow	Vice-Provost, Faculty Group of Arts, Divinity and Music, The University of Edinburgh
Dr Fred Forster	Co-Director, TLA Centre, The University of Edinburgh
Dr Dai Hounsell	Co-Director, TLA Centre, The University of Edinburgh
Dr Miesbeth Knottenbelt	Development Officer, TLA Centre, The University of Edinburgh
Mrs Sheila Thompson	Research Associate, TLA Centre, The University of Edinburgh
Dr DES Truman	Vice-Dean, Faculty Group of Science and Engineering, The University of Edinburgh

Layout and Formatting

Mrs Jenny Hounsell	Administrator, TLA Centre, The University of Edinburgh

Cover Design

Mr Alan Perris	Senior Designer, Visual Resources, The University of Edinburgh

Chapter 1

Introduction

Fred Forster, Dai Hounsell and Sheila Thompson

Tutoring and demonstrating play well-established and fundamentally important parts in undergraduate teaching, especially in the formative first and second years of the undergraduate curriculum. Within the setting of a small group, tutorials and practical classes enable students to deepen and extend their understanding of material introduced in lectures or seminars. Equally importantly, they provide a bridge to independent study, helping students to consolidate what they have learnt through wider reading and assigned coursework. These classes also serve as direct points of contact with a particular member of the teaching staff, avoiding the impersonality and sense of isolation which might otherwise arise at a time when student numbers – and class sizes – have grown substantially.

In the 1990s, tutoring and demonstrating responsibilities are increasingly being taken up by part-time teaching staff: postgraduate research students, graduate teaching assistants, postdoctoral fellows, graduate professionals (such as practising lawyers and accountants) and teaching fellows with relevant postgraduate qualifications. If they are to perform their roles as tutors or demonstrators effectively, however, these part-time staff need to be adequately briefed, trained and supported. This handbook is intended to make a key contribution to that end, and can usefully complement departmental briefing seminars, faculty or university-wide workshops, and course-based support systems. Although written chiefly with new part-time teaching staff in mind, the handbook should also be helpful to many others: to more experienced tutors and demonstrators, and to the lecturers and course organisers who are their course team colleagues.

CONTENT AND STRUCTURE

The contents of the handbook have been tailored broadly to the needs of new tutors and demonstrators in universities. The handbook does not address teaching practices within individual departments, nor could it realistically seek to do so given the range of disciplines involved and their distinctive approaches to teaching and learning. The handbook is therefore a complement to departmentally based briefing, training and support.

The eleven chapters which follow can be seen as falling into three main parts. The first group of chapters provides an orientation to tutoring and demonstrating and examines the main areas of day-to-day practice.

- *Chapter 2* presents an overview of the different roles and responsibilities and suggests how new staff might begin to go about learning the ropes.

- *Chapter 3* outlines what is involved both in preparing for and in conducting tutorial classes in the arts and social sciences.

- *Chapter 4* focuses on tutoring of problem-solving classes in mathematics and the sciences.

- *Chapter 5* reviews demonstrating practice in laboratory and field classes in the sciences including marking of practical work.

- *Chapter 6* reviews the tutor's role in relation to coursework essays and offers guidance on marking students' written work and on giving constructive feedback.

- *Chapter 7* broadens out the themes of guidance and support, looking at what can be done during classes and in one-to-one discussion with students.

Next there is *Chapter 8*, which reviews some of the key research findings on student learning. This chapter has a crucial bridging function. On the one hand, it provides a theoretical underpinning to the first group of chapters. On the other, it explores ideas and insights which can inform the chapters which follow, each of which addresses ways in which part-time staff can enhance their effectiveness.

- *Chapter 9* points up the benefits of working with a mentor and of sharing ideas and experiences with other tutors and demonstrators.

- *Chapter 10* outlines a range of methods for getting feedback on one's teaching and suggests how feedback information can be analysed and applied.

- *Chapter 11* argues for the adoption of a reflective approach to practice and indicates some possible ways of doing this.

- *Chapter 12* is a compendium of sources of information and advice on which tutors and demonstrators can draw for their own needs or those of their students.

This three-fold chapter structure therefore progresses from practical matters through theoretical perspectives to developmental concerns. Nonetheless, the chapters have been designed to be read independently as well as sequentially, since it is recognised that staff will approach their reading of the handbook from a variety of different standpoints. Some will want to make practicalities their priority, dipping into whichever of the early chapters will best prepare them for the particular role they have been assigned. Others may prefer to see theory as their chosen avenue towards practice, by beginning with chapter 8, *Student Learning*.

At key points throughout the handbook, readers are invited to consider how they might apply what is being discussed to their own particular circumstances within a specific course and departmental setting. Working through these activities can be an effective way to begin to put into practice many of the ideas, principles and strategies presented in the handbook. Where appropriate, suggestions for further reading are included at the end of chapters.

Chapter 2
Roles and Responsibilities
Frances Dow and DES Truman

INTRODUCTION

Many universities are privileged to have a large community of active, committed postgraduate students who are willing to undertake part-time teaching duties. Many are also in the fortunate position of being able to draw on other suitably qualified members of their local community, for example, clinicians and practising lawyers and accountants, to undertake part-time teaching roles. In a time of scarce resources, the contribution which these tutors, demonstrators, and other part-time staff make to the teaching provision of a university is not just valuable : it is vital. Without it, we would not be able to maintain the quality of the teaching which is such a distinctive feature of UK higher education.

In any resource scenario, the standard and type of teaching which is offered to undergraduate students would be much diminished if tutors and demonstrators were not involved, for they can often fulfil some roles much more satisfactorily than more senior staff. Of course, their principal roles are the ones they share with all other teaching staff. There is, first, the academic role of supporting and enhancing student learning and, second, the pastoral role of enabling students to deal with their own personal and welfare concerns. Both of these are examined more fully in the rest of this chapter. But in addition, postgraduate tutors and demonstrators can have a special 'bridging' role to play between the worlds of teaching and research, and they can often be very effective role models for first-degree students.

Many universities in their mission statements have committed themselves to sustaining and developing teaching in a research-led environment, and it can often be postgraduates who, in their daily working lives, do most to bring these two aspects of universities' work together. This is not because postgraduates are expected to make their research

topics the focus of teaching - far from it - but because the commitment and enthusiasm which they bring to teaching is so very often a reflection of their intense interest in furthering knowledge and the understanding of it through research.

They, much more than other staff members who are not so continuously active in research because of heavier teaching or administrative burdens, can give undergraduates an immediate sense of the excitement of discovery and of what it means to be at the cutting-edge of research. Thus, even though they have not been part of the academic world for as long as senior staff, postgraduate tutors and demonstrators are particularly good models for bringing home to others the importance of academic values and aspirations. In other words, they show very clearly what a university is 'about'. Not all tutors and demonstrators are postgraduates, however. Many are drawn from the professions and thus provide a different, but equally important, bridge between the worlds of academic knowledge and day-to-day professional practice.

In fulfilling these roles, part-time teachers do not - and certainly should not - act alone, nor should they imagine that there are no limits or boundaries to their responsibilities. In the academic and the pastoral roles especially, it is the student, and not the tutor, who has the ultimate responsibility for his or her own learning and personal welfare. In performing their duties, tutors and demonstrators can also expect support and help from the department in which they teach, and the next section in this chapter looks in more detail at the division of responsibilities between part-time staff and other members of their departments and universities.

In the remainder of the chapter there is a short section on the tutor's and demonstrator's responsibilities in relation to devising a teaching programme, followed by another on problems associated with marking and assessment. Then the pastoral role is looked at briefly, and the chapter concludes by suggesting how part-time staff might begin to reflect on their personal priorities as they embark upon their teaching responsibilities.

PART-TIME TEACHING STAFF AND THE DEPARTMENTS

When any part-time tutor or demonstrator agrees to take on teaching duties in a department, that department has a responsibility to define the extent of these duties, and also to formalise arrangements concerning pay and hours of work. This is simply good professional practice, and no one should feel hesitant in asking for the following aspects of his or her responsibilities to be clarified in the form of a job description (see *figure 1* for an example). If things are clear from the outset, it will help the part-time teacher orient him or herself in the life of the department and set up a good working relationship with other teaching staff.

• All tutors and demonstrators should be given a formal letter of appointment from the head of department or other organisation responsible for the teaching, and this should state the number of contact hours and the rate of pay. This rate may vary depending on the exact nature of the duties, and differs between tutors

and demonstrators. Payment for giving a formal lecture (not normally asked of postgraduate tutors) is set at a higher rate than the standard tutorial rate, and this in turn is higher than the payment for certain types of language teaching for which little preparation is needed. The standard tutorial rate includes an element for preparation and other associated duties, as well as the actual contact hour, while the payment for demonstrators is solely for contact hours, on the grounds that the preparation required for demonstrating is significantly less than that for tutoring.

• Departments must spell out clearly which, if any, duties are associated with the teaching (practice will vary across an institution), and in particular they should make clear to tutors and demonstrators whether marking or other forms of assessment is included. If there is a requirement for the tutor to be available at set times to students for consultation, this should be taken into consideration in calculating payment.

• Part-time teaching staff should also be informed of how they will be paid - at the end of each term is usual, but some departments may pay twice termly.

All this enables the part-time teacher to be sure that

ARTIFICIAL INTELLIGENCE DEPARTMENT - JOB DESCRIPTIONS
(kept on-line and mailed to potential tutors/demonstrators)

Course: AI1   *Level*:   FIRST YEAR

Course Organisers:

Type of Job: GENERAL TUTOR

Number of Contact Hours: 1 per week, 22 in total (8/9/5 for each term)

Number of Tutors Needed: 9/10 (c. 8 per tutor)

Short Course Description: The course is an introductory one, assuming no prior experience. The modules cover Prolog, Natural Language, Problem Solving, Vision, Current Issues and Philosophical Issues plus an introduction to Symbolic Computation. Each student writes an essay in term 1 and another essay or a project in term 2. The class is a mixture of Arts (mostly Linguistics), Social Science (mostly Psychology) and Science students (more than half the class are first year Computer Science students). Tutors look after a group of about 8 students over the academic year and are their main contact with the A.I. Department, and the department's main contact with the students.

Specific Requirements: An ability to communicate with students who know nothing about A.I., and to appreciate their difficulties and misunderstandings. A general background in A.I. - sufficient to keep 2 steps ahead of the students in each of the above modules. Essay topics, tutorial assignments and reading assignments are set by lecturers. General tutors are mainly responsible for: tutoring students on A.I. and on general study skills; monitoring attendance and general progress of students; supervising essay and project writing. Additionally tutors are required to give the students feedback on a number of assigned tutorial exercises and reading assignments, and to be involved in the marking of essays and projects. (Note: marking by postgraduates will be supervised and additional payments will be made at the rate of one hour of marking per week, averaged over 22 weeks).

Figure 1[1]

---

he or she is really willing to undertake duties on these terms, and once agreed, these are binding on both parties.

- Departments should also tell tutors and demonstrators what training they are required to undertake and where and by whom this is to be delivered.

- In allocating teaching hours to part-time staff, departments are expected to take into account their other commitments, especially research. Many departments will allow tutors to choose their own teaching hours, and so plan their own timetable, but sometimes constraints on the availability of accommodation or the fixity of a class hour make this impossible. A tutor should be told how much freedom he or she has to set class times. Departments are expected to avoid undue fragmentation of a tutor's timetable, so that the uninterrupted blocks of time which are necessary for research and writing, and also for teaching preparation, are not constantly disrupted. Laboratory and field-work demonstrators will generally be working to a specified time-table.

- Most especially, in the case of postgraduates, departments should not expect tutors to teach in more than one or two courses unless their expertise is particularly widespread, because this adds significantly to the burden of preparation.

It is worth noting here that, when the course is underway, all teaching staff have a responsibility to turn up promptly at the appointed times. Illness apart, they must not miss or cancel classes. If special circumstances make it desirable to rearrange a class hour either to suit the tutor (who might, say, have to attend a training session) or the students (who might perhaps want to attend a special lecture), this will usually be acceptable, so long as the department knows and the students themselves agree and clearly understand the alternative arrangements.

- It is common practice for a university to require departments to nominate a member of the lecturing staff to whom the tutor or demonstrator is responsible, and from whom he or she can seek help and advice. This may be a course leader or it may be another member of staff with knowledge and experience of the course in which the teaching takes place. The tutor's or demonstrator's formal responsibility to this person is rather different from his or her relationship with a 'mentor', who is an experienced senior academic who acts more

informally as a guide or support to a tutor in developing his or her professional expertise. Mentoring schemes are becoming more widespread and where they do exist departments should inform tutors about them, and how they function.

- If marking or other forms of assessment are included in the duties, the department must give clear guidance on the marking scale and the assessment criteria to be used. A tutor will be given advice, especially if marking essays for the first time, and the person to whom he or she is responsible (as well, possibly, as the mentor) will supervise or monitor his or her marking. Corresponding arrangements will be made where demonstrators are involved in assessing laboratory or field work. In many courses or departments, all staff contributing to a course are involved in a similar process of moderation or standardisation of their marks.

- Advice and help on assessment should include a clear statement of the department's policy on granting extensions to deadlines for written work and penalties for late submission of essays etc. In similar vein, departments should tell part-time staff if there are formal requirements to report a student's non-attendance at classes to the appropriate person.

- Departments must also attend to the practical details which allow teaching to take place. They must allocate teaching space for tutors and provide the same level of secretarial support as they give other teaching staff to ease communication with students and course leaders. They must issue curricular materials (such as course booklets and laboratory guides) and give practical information on things such as photocopying procedures. Should appropriate teaching materials not be provided, the tutor should contact the course leader.

- Perhaps most importantly, the course leader, or another member of the department with first-hand experience of the relevant course(s), must discuss with tutors how much autonomy they have in devising their own tutorial programme and what constraints there are on what and how to teach. More is said about this in the next section.

Setting out responsibilities has advantages both for the department and the tutor or demonstrator. It sets their employment in a proper professional context, and it allows the department to be sure that the quality of teaching provision for its undergraduate students is maintained. It also ensures that an adequate framework is in place for the department to be able to say to the part-time teacher "over to you", and for the tutor or demonstrator to respond with confidence, when teaching gets under way.

> *The above review has identified a number of roles you will have as a tutor or demonstrator and some of the principal responsibilities associated with each. Some of the avenues by which you might take things forward have also been indicated.*
>
> *What seem to be early priorities for you to get to grips with - and how will you make a start?*

THE TEACHING PROGRAMME

Tutoring

Although universities are convinced of the essential value of tutorials in fostering undergraduates' critical and creative thinking in relation to their chosen discipline(s), they also recognise that tutorials can achieve a multiplicity of aims and that there is therefore no one thing that tutorials are 'for'. In general, however, tutorials must integrate with and enhance the structure, content and aims of the course of which they are a part, and so in the most basic sense all tutors must, in developing their tutorial programme, 'follow the course'.

What this means in practice, and in particular how much autonomy this allows tutors to devise their own programme, will differ from course to course, even within the same department. As noted above, this is an important subject for discussion and negotiation between course leader and tutor before the course begins. It is an important part of the responsibilities of tutors to ensure that they have identified, understood and accepted the constraints under which they will work. If they do not, their students may suffer, for when it comes to formal assessment some students may find themselves less well prepared than others if their tutors have not developed a tutorial programme which relates to the main features of the course. It is very likely, however, that tutors will find the structure of a course sufficiently flexible to give them some opportunity (and in many cases, considerable opportunity) to use their own distinctive ideas, interests, experience and expertise in their teaching.

More advice on how to go about planning tutorials which relate to the overall structure of the course

as well as to the tutor's own interests and expertise is given in chapter 3 on *Tutoring in Arts and Social Sciences*. This also discusses some of the basic aims of tutorials, which can include

* deepening knowledge;

* problem-solving;

* facilitating open-ended exploration of themes and issues;

* developing skills in argumentation and communication.

When it comes to taking the tutorial, tutors have a responsibility for what happens 'in the classroom'. This means that they are responsible for identifying the purpose of a tutorial and for their own style in fulfilling that purpose. They are responsible for leading the group, and for managing group interaction, to achieve this end. But they cannot dictate what the quality of that interaction will be, and their teaching skills are only one factor in influencing the outcome of any tutorial. All teaching staff find that, even when the topic, the method and the tutor are the same, no two tutorial groups are alike because each teaching and learning experience is the product of the interaction of the whole group, not just a reflection of the skills of the tutor.

Important as tutors are, it is good to remember that they are not responsible for the students' learning: the students are responsible for that. In other words, the tutor's basic responsibility is to create a good learning environment for the students, not to try to do the students' learning for them.

Each university and its constituent departments therefore have some very basic expectations of how tutors will approach their teaching duties, but there is no template for what in detail they should do. This makes it both easier and harder for the tutor. On the one hand, there may be considerable freedom to develop one's own interests, impart one's own enthusiasms and cultivate one's own style. The other side of the coin is that the multiplicity of choice as to what to do and how to do it means there is no 'right' answer to some of the questions involved in teaching, although the chapters in this handbook should provide some guidance.

Such hard-and-fast 'rules' as there are for part-time tutors relate to their obligation to fulfil the terms of the initial agreement with the department, and also to their duty to maintain a fair, impartial and professional relationship with undergraduate students. This is important for both the student and the tutor at all times.

Demonstrating

The flexibility available to the demonstrator in the laboratory is generally much less than that which exists in a tutorial. The programme of work in the laboratory or in the field is usually determined in a fairly specific way by the full-time member of teaching staff responsible. Nevertheless, the interaction between the demonstrator and students has an element of personal contact which is greatly valued by students. In some cases students may find it easier to admit their difficulties to a demonstrator than to the full-time academic staff involved in the course. It is particularly important that the demonstrator is active in making contact with students and does not merely wait for questions to be asked. For example, the demonstrator should be willing to ask questions of the students to discover the extent of their understanding. It may be helpful for the staff running laboratory classes to suggest questions that demonstrators might ask.

Part-time demonstrators are not expected necessarily to be familiar with all the techniques and material covered in a laboratory class before they embark on demonstrating, but where they are not it is important that they should familiarise themselves with the material before the start of the practical class. Briefing meetings are often held to help prepare demonstrators for a particular class and all such meetings should be attended. The aims of the practical class and the nature of the material will be covered in such briefings. Where there are particular aspects of safety to be considered, it is vital that demonstrators are fully competent; the demonstrator is a crucial link between the member of full-time staff running the class and the students carrying out the practical work. Chapter 5 reviews demonstrating practice in laboratory and field work classes in more detail.

MARKING AND ASSESSMENT

The extent to which postgraduate and other part-time tutors and demonstrators are involved in assessing students' coursework varies between courses. Part-time teaching staff are not usually given formal status as members of Boards of Examiners or asked to mark degree examinations, but in many, probably most, departments it is common for them to be asked to mark essays or other exercises which are part of the written requirements of the course throughout the year.

If a tutor is involved in marking, this gives him or her first-hand experience of an important dimension to the student's learning, and it is of great benefit to the student to be given feedback on coursework from the same person who is involved in other aspects of the teaching/learning programme.

All departments must ensure that part-time teaching staff know and understand the assessment criteria and the marking scale in use in the relevant course. Tutors and demonstrators should feel free to ask for a detailed explanation of what is intended by the criteria - simply to be given a written copy of the marking scale is not likely to be enough. The department also has a responsibility to make arrangements for the checking and moderating of all staff marking, in the interests of quality assurance. This may involve the double-marking of some or all of the written exercises for students in a given group or class. In the case of part-time staff marking for the first time, the course leader or another experienced colleague should give fuller preliminary guidance, and go over samples of the tutor's marking at an early stage.

Tutors and demonstrators are responsible for adhering to the assessment guidelines and the marking scale in use in the course, and for submitting samples of their marking as required for moderation, double-marking etc. They must also check that they are fulfilling the administrative work associated with marking, e.g. handing in marks to the course leader or departmental secretary for recording and collation.

Fuller advice on marking and related tasks is given in chapter 6, *Marking and Commenting on Essays*, and within chapter 5 on demonstrating. But it is worth saying here that the responsibility of marking involves more than 'giving a mark' to students' work. The assessment process should help students advance their learning and improve their understanding, and so the comments and feedback which are given to students are just as important as the actual mark. For example, it is useful to give some of this feedback in writing – a few paragraphs at the end of an essay, perhaps – but many students will also want a face-to-face discussion. At least some of this can be done by using the regular tutorial hour for giving back essays individually.

Tutors and demonstrators, however, should not feel that students can make unlimited demands on their time and expertise when it comes to coping with written work. It is part of a teacher's function to give guidance and support in report- and essay-writing to improve students' skills. But again it should be emphasised that students have responsibility for their own learning, and it is not the responsibility of tutors to do students' written work for them. So, for example, the tutor is not expected to look at several redrafts of an essay or to go over a written exercise time and time again. To end up in a situation where the tutor has put as much into the task as the student is not in the long term helpful to the student, and, however well-intentioned, it is not part of the tutor's professional duties.

In laboratory teaching and fieldwork much of the feedback to students provided by demonstrators will be oral, given while the work is being carried out. If laboratory or fieldwork reports are to be marked, demonstrators should seek guidance on how much detail is expected to be provided by way of written feedback to students.

THE PASTORAL ROLE

The pastoral role of the part-time teacher is another area where there are limits to what can and should be done. This is to their benefit as well as the students'. Not all teaching staff agree on how the limits should be defined, but in essence most accept that staff should not go outside a professional relationship with their students, both in terms of the time and the sympathy and degree of involvement which they give to students' personal problems. Tutors and demonstrators must not infringe the students' ultimate responsibility for resolving their own personal or welfare concerns. Laboratory or fieldwork demonstrators are perhaps less likely than tutors to be given a pastoral responsibility for students, but should this happen, then the same considerations outlined above would apply.

Tutors and demonstrators should remain receptive to the student who really does need guidance, even if they have no personal sympathy with the particular problem. A problem will very often be simple and short-lived, and it is entirely appropriate for teachers to help simply by listening, and so help the student clarify the nature of his or her concern.

Striking a balance may be quite tricky, especially for part-time teachers whose age and role in the academic community often makes them seem more approachable than older, more senior members of staff. What really matters is watching out for problems which can have a serious adverse impact

on academic functioning, and knowing who else in the student support system (e.g. personal tutor or university counselling or health service) needs to be brought in, and when. There is usually an established network of services on which tutors can draw for their students' benefit, and more is said about this in chapter 7, *Supporting and Advising Students*.

Many student problems are first manifested in non-attendance at classes and the tutor should watch out for this as a warning sign. Generally, institutions require repeated non-attendance to be reported to the course leader or to the student's personal tutor. With regard to absence from practical classes, the demonstrator may have a role in reporting this to the member of academic staff or technician in charge of the class. These mechanisms allow other agencies to be brought in to help deal with the problem.

Sometimes tutors or demonstrators may feel a tension between their pastoral responsibility towards one student and their more general duty to implement departmental policy on, say, penalties for late work or non-attendance at class. Especially if a student has spoken in confidence, it may be difficult to know how and when to pass information on to another colleague. If possible the nature and extent of the confidentiality should have been discussed with the student at the time. It may be useful to distinguish between making known the fact of a student's non-compliance with course requirements and divulging the reasons behind it. The latter should normally be disclosed only with the student's permission and/or after the matter has been discussed with the student as being in his or her best interest.

Part-time staff may find it helpful to talk over 'problem' cases with a more experienced colleague, preserving the student's anonymity if necessary. It may also help to reflect on one's responsibility to all students, not just to a single one, and to ask if special allowances made to one student, say for non-production of work, undermine the achievements of the others who have striven to meet the deadlines, etc.

CONCLUSION

This overview has tried to show what universities expect of their part-time teaching staff and how these expectations fit in with the responsibilities of the department, on the one hand, and the undergraduate student on the other. It is the department, and behind it the individual schools or faculties, which are responsible for defining the parameters of the part-time teacher's role and duties, and for giving him or her sufficient information and practical support to allow teaching to take place. But the tutor or demonstrator has the responsibility for deciding how to flesh out and execute that role, and how to fulfil these responsibilities in such a way as to enhance the undergraduate's learning experience. The contributors to this handbook hope that the

following chapters will help part-time staff develop their own teaching style and derive enjoyment and satisfaction from their much valued contribution to teaching provision in universities.

FOOTNOTES

1. With kind permission of the Department of Artificial Intelligence, The University of Edinburgh.

Chapter 3

Tutoring in Arts and Social Sciences

Fred Forster

INTRODUCTION

Tutorial classes, in which a small group of students meets with a tutor on a regular basis play a well-established and crucial part in the quality of undergraduate learning in the arts and social sciences. The broad purpose of these classes, as indicated in chapter 2, *Roles and Responsibilities*, is to help students consolidate and extend their learning beyond that acquired from other parts of their courses, notably from lectures and private study.

This developmental process has two aspects which are intimately connected. Tutorials are used to promote students' further understanding of the concepts, theories, facts and procedures which make up the core of a subject. Additionally, they provide opportunities for encouraging students to develop those critical and creative thinking skills and forms of expression and argument which are characteristic of a particular academic discipline. Thus, tutorials enable students to become more knowledgeable about subject-matter but also to develop the facility for using their knowledge in the manner of the disciplinary practitioner – for example, to think and argue as a language specialist, a musician or sociologist as the case may be.

The potential that tutorials have for developing these aspects of learning lies in the opportunities they provide for students to work actively and cooperatively with their peers and tutors – something which is largely missing from lectures and private study. Tutors are thus well placed, indeed uniquely so, to assist their students to develop those higher-order intellectual functions which are at the heart of a university undergraduate education. They do so in a number of ways.

- By drawing on their subject expertise, tutors set learning tasks for students, monitor what they make of them and respond accordingly.

- Through skills of group management, tutors can encourage students to take an active part in the group and so learn from the other students as well as the tutor.

- By exercising self awareness, tutors can judge the fine line that lies between, on the one hand, contributing their subject insights to the work of the class and, on the other, so dominating the group that students are denied the space to take responsibility for their own learning.

Thus the tutor contributes to the tutorial class from two perspectives simultaneously – as subject expert and as facilitator of the students' learning.

This chapter is primarily concerned with some of the practical issues which tutors address as they prepare for and conduct tutorial classes. In particular, it draws attention to a range of strategies and tactics which they may find useful for their own tutorial circumstances. It is assumed that tutors will be dealing with inexperienced undergraduates, that they are to conduct a series of tutorials on a regular basis, such as weekly or fortnightly, and that they have considerable discretion over the pattern of learning activities that will take place during classes and also in preparation for them.

The material in the chapter is organised into three sections which mirror the principal emphases in the concerns of tutors as they move from appointment through an orientation phase, meet with the students for the first time and pass on to the mainstream of their tutorial classes. Tutors are invited to:

- clarify some key issues which have a bearing on the selection of tasks for tutorials and on their approach to management of the group

- consider in detail the first meeting they take with a class

- review some of the practicalities of preparing for and conducting tutorials.

Whilst written principally for tutors in the humanities and social sciences, much of the material is relevant to other disciplines in higher education.

FINDING ONE'S BEARINGS

Understandably, most tutors wish to develop an early feeling of security about their dual role as a subject authority and a leader of a learning group. Clarifying the following issues can give tutors some early confidence:

- the nature of academic discourse in their discipline;

- the subject-matter for their tutorials;

- the learning aims for their tutorials;

- the importance of student participation.

All of these issues have a bearing on how tutors approach and deliver tutorials. Thinking them through will give tutors a set of frameworks against which to select relevant subject-matter, to devise and sequence appropriate learning tasks and to choose methods of working which will encourage active involvement by students.

Academic Discourse[1]

Having been successful undergraduates and having begun to develop their specialist postgraduate studies, tutors will already be familiar with the intellectual processes and nature of academic argument in their disciplines. As a principal purpose of tutorials is to inculcate these habits of thought and practice in students, tutors may find revisiting them reassuring. Clarifying these perspectives with a mentor, a course leader or other colleague may help tutors appreciate how much more they are likely to know about these fundamental matters than beginning under-graduates. Hopefully they will come to see that they are in fact better equipped to approach their tutoring duties than they perhaps feel at the outset.

What do you see as the principal intellectual skills that your subject area requires? It may be helpful to contrast your own subject with another with which you have some familiarity.

Getting to Grips with the Subject-Matter

An early concern for many tutors is to understand the subject matter to be covered in their classes.

Chapter 7, *Supporting and Advising Students*, outlines a number of ways they can go about tuning in to details of course structure, content and what it is that is required of students. Here we are only concerned with tutors acquiring an understanding of the essential subject-matter needed to conduct tutorials. Probably the most efficient way of getting to grips with this is to attend the students' lecture course(s), time permitting. But even where this is possible, tutors may find it helpful to have copies of the basic texts and additional recommended reading materials. These are needed both as information sources and as resources for the setting of tasks.

The question of what depth of knowledge is needed to be able to tutor effectively is one that causes a lot of concern. Some very anxious tutors become so concerned at the thought of being unable to answer students' questions that they resort to encyclopaedic preparation in a vain attempt to cover every eventuality. Clearly, a minimum is to be well acquainted with the sources and course material that the students are studying. In some subjects this may mean a deep immersion in detail – for example where technical accuracy is required as in translation of foreign languages.

Drawing the line at what it is useful to know, however, is very difficult. Some feel for where the limits lie may perhaps be gained by considering how tutors use their subject knowledge to support their students' efforts to learn in tutorials. They do so in broadly three ways:

- They draw on their knowledge to devise learning tasks such as setting a passage for translation, selecting a topic as a discussion focus, choosing a chapter of a text for detailed reading, selecting a piece of music for listening to and comment ...

- As students disclose in tutorials what they make of the task, tutors register this against their own knowledge and in turn respond – perhaps, for example, to encourage students to do further exploration of the topic.

- They may respond directly to queries from students.

Tutors who feel confident about setting tasks and listening to and responding to students' exchanges will usually know enough to answer most student queries. Occasionally, however, a tutor will be stumped and some suggestions for how to respond in this situation are given on page 17.

Finally, tutors need to be alert to a specific hazard which attends excessive preparation. The danger is that a tutor may feel driven to justify the investment of preparation time by moving centre stage with his/her own material to a degree which denies the students space to contribute.

Clarifying Aims

Learning aims are statements of intent which indicate in a general sense what it is that students are meant to achieve. Some of the principal aims pursued in tutorials are shown in *table 1* with examples of the learning that students might do in pursuit of each.

Aims help tutors by providing a clear guide to the learning focus and hence to choosing appropriate learning tasks. For example, if the development of students' verbal communication skills is the aim, then suitable learning tasks might be for students to present papers, to chair discussions, to engage in a debate, to offer summaries of discussions and so on.

Making the aims explicit for a series of tutorials and for each individual session within it can be very helpful to students too. This can assist them to see the essential purpose for a tutorial and so meet with a shared understanding of common purpose. Without this, individuals might work to their own

SOME LEARNING AIMS FOR TUTORIAL GROUPS

Aim	Examples
1. UNDERSTANDING *Helping students to consolidate and enhance their understanding of a subject or discipline*	• clarifying concepts, theories and procedures • reflecting on inter-connections • testing their understanding through examples, cases, illustrations
2. CRITICAL THINKING *Helping students to develop their capacity for thinking critically and analytically*	• reviewing evidence in the light of theories • learning how to 'set' and solve problems or approach questions and issues • enhancing their capacity for logical reasoning and formal argument
3. PERSONAL GROWTH *Helping students to develop and mature as individuals*	• clarifying attitudes, articulating and reappraising values • developing in self-confidence and self-esteem • evolving a sense of responsibility and commitment
4. COMMUNICATION SKILLS *Helping students to learn how to communicate effectively with others*	• refining listening, questioning and explaining skills • presenting and defending a position clearly and cogently • giving and getting feedback
5. GROUP AND TEAMWORK SKILLS *Helping students to learn how to collaborate and work as an effective group or team*	• setting, allocating and monitoring tasks • supporting and encouraging other members of the group or team • initiating, directing and leading tasks
6. SELF-DIRECTION IN LEARNING *Helping students to take progressively greater responsibility for their learning*	• clarifying their own goals as learners • managing their study time and effort and setting priorities • accepting responsibility for evaluating their own work and their progress as learners

Table 1

unspecified aims and agendas to the detriment of cohesive learning in the group.

Which learning aims have priority will usually be made clear by the department. In practice, most tutors will follow a combination of those shown in *table 1*. The fact that multiple aims are often pursued is another very important reason for making them explicit as students may otherwise miss the essential point. As an example, understanding subject content is almost always a major tutorial aim. But the second aim in *table 1*, critical thinking, may have a higher priority. In the absence of clear guidance about this, weaker students especially may continue to believe that, as at school, understanding the facts is the ultimate goal. Aims then are a fundamental issue; clarifying which ones have priority for a tutorial series is one of the ways in which tutors can begin to feel that their initial orientations are soundly based.

Looking ahead to your tutorial classes, which of the learning aims in table 1 will be most relevant to your students?

Are there any additional aims that might be important?

Encouraging Participation

The information in *table 1* will alert tutors to the need for students to be active in tutorials if such aims are to be achieved. It is through the linked processes of thinking and communicating amongst the members of the group that students' intellectual and social skills are sharpened and attitudes are clarified, challenged and perhaps modified, whilst at the same time knowledge of the subject matter is consolidated and extended.

Tutors can do a lot to help these sophisticated learning processes come about by taking steps to create a positive and cooperative climate for learning in the group. This needs to be addressed overtly because a lot of new undergraduates may be reluctant initially to participate in a group setting. Some students arrive at university brimming with confidence, but tutors can hardly assume that this will be the norm. Others will be unaware of the purpose and value of tutorials; few will have a clear understanding of discussion skills – fewer still will be practised in their use. Also, many new students, doubting they could have much of value to say, will

feel obliged to view the tutor as an expert to whom they should defer. Additionally, others will see the tutor as an assessor and be inhibited from expressing views by this. A considerable number may also be confused by having to work together in tutorials and will need encouragement to do so. Indeed it is easy to forget they are in a setting where marks matter and they are in competition for these. Clearly tutors need to anticipate these kinds of issues and plan to deal with them from the start. What then makes for effective student participation in tutorials?

Figure 1 lists some of the factors which can encourage students to take part in tutorials. There are a number of implications here for tutors as few of these desirable conditions are likely to exist when a first year tutorial group first meets. Initially, measures are required to encourage individual students to grow in confidence and also to help

---

ENCOURAGING STUDENTS TO CONTRIBUTE

Students are encouraged to contribute in tutorials when:

- they feel comfortable with each other and the tutor

- trust and respect are displayed and support is given

- learning is seen as a cooperative exercise

- there is a clear understanding of what they have to learn

- they are aware of the importance of participation

- they are aware of the skills which they are expected to practise

- students are set realistic and achievable tasks

- methods are used in early tutorials which foster students' contributions

- ground rules have been agreed, e.g.

  – everyone prepares and attends

  – everyone tries to contribute and helps others to do so

Figure 1

---

establish an early climate of trust as members of a group with a remit to work together. Though these processes have to be worked at over a period of time, tutors can go a long way to fostering them during the early meetings of the class through the use of appropriate methods. Some examples of useful approaches are given below in the review of the first meeting of the class.

A further implication is the need to make explicit to students what is expected of them. Usually *what* they are to learn is made clear but making clear *how* the learning is to be achieved is also important. Students are more likely to contribute in the group for example, if they are made aware of the skills they can use in discussion. The initial meeting of the tutorial group is therefore a critical one for laying some of these foundations. In the next section we focus on this meeting, reviewing some of the key purposes it can serve and drawing attention to some strategies which tutors might use to get the group off to a good start.

MAKING A GOOD START

It is important that the first meeting goes well – for students and tutor alike. If the experience is a favourable one, this will act as a spur to student motivation and attendance at the following sessions.

The underlying purpose is to get the students and tutor to take the first steps towards functioning as a learning group. To this end, some important aims are to begin to:

* develop in students a respect for serious academic work;

* foster a spirit of cooperation and collaboration;

and for the tutor there is also a need to:

* develop confidence in the dual role of subject expert and facilitator of the group.

These purposes suggest a balanced agenda between business items and activities aimed at establishing a positive climate for learning. Because this meeting is an introduction to a series there are usually a considerable number of administrative and procedural matters to deal with. Of necessity, these will be tutor-led. Counterbalancing these with activities which will involve students as contributors is critical. Students' expectations for the tutorial series will be shaped in part by what happens to them during the first meeting. If they leave having had opportunities to participate and having had their contributions valued, then

significant groundwork will have been laid on which to build later.

Naturally, the precise form an agenda takes for this meeting, the detailed activities it contains and their sequencing, will vary with the subject and course. Below are some key ideas which tutors may find they can use directly or adapt for their own situation. In practice, social convention usually exerts a pressure to begin with introductions of group members to each other.

Getting to Know Each Other

In everyday life we find it easier to talk to people we know than to strangers. Tutorials are no exception. Learning each others' names and perhaps a little about each other is a helpful way to begin to establish relationships. Inviting students to join with you in making introductions to one another (or to members of a sub-group if the class is a big one) ensures every student says something and begins to establish a presence in the group. This process takes only a few minutes and everyone will contribute given a few moments of private reflection to pull together one or two personal points to share.

Can you think of other ways in which you could help students in a group to get to know each other better? Various techniques for 'ice-breaking' as it is sometimes called are included in many of the books about teaching groups.[2]

Establishing an Intellectual Climate

Students will expect the tutor to brief them about the work that the group will undertake and also what is expected of them. This gives an early opportunity to begin to establish a climate of serious academic intent by:

* explaining the aims of the tutorial series;

* making explicit the roles and responsibilities of members of the group including the tutor;

* reviewing the skills needed for effective participation;

* giving guidance about preparation for the following tutorial.

Making Aims Explicit. It can be helpful to provide students with a written statement of the learning aims for the tutorials, as it can be all too easy for a verbal briefing about such issues to be forgotten. It can also be useful to tell students how these learning aims complement those which apply to lectures and other learning activities such as self-study. They will then see how the different strands of their learning contribute to their intellectual development and this may influence their behaviour – for example, if they know that tutorials are meant to build on concepts and arguments introduced in lectures and they see that this is adhered to in practice, this can reinforce their motivation to attend lectures and tutorials.

Making Roles and Responsibilities Clear. Establishing a clear understanding of the aims for the tutorials clears the ground for a review of the methods that will be used in the group and of who will be responsible for what. If students know that a prime purpose of attending tutorials is to develop intellectual skills of analysing information and appropriate communication skills of argument, they will more readily see the value of their two-fold responsibilities to do preparatory work and to come to tutorials prepared to take part in discussion.

It is important that tutors make clear their own positions. Informing students they will fulfil different roles in the group as circumstances require, for example acting as chairman of discussions, as manager of the group, as occasional contributor and so on, reinforces the point that the learning outcomes will hinge primarily upon the students' own efforts.

Skills for Student Participation. Reviewing roles and responsibilities will highlight for students the importance of participation in tutorial classes and the need for understanding the skills they can use in their particular academic setting. *Figure 2* lists some of the skills which are relevant to a discussion class.

Reviewing these skills can be very reassuring for beginning students. For example, knowing that it is legitimate and helpful to ask for clarification when puzzled, or to concur with a point made by another student by offering a supportive example of one's own, can do a lot to reduce anxiety. Lacking this kind of information, some students will imagine that tutorial discussions are about the sharing of rarefied insights – which they know they rarely possess – and so become discouraged. By dispelling such myths, tutors can do much to bolster the fragile confidence of beginning students.

Setting Preparation. Tutors can send a strong signal about the serious professional work of the tutorial group by specifically setting preparation for the

---

SKILLS FOR PARTICIPATING

- Listening attentively to others.

- Giving information to others.

- Asking others for information.

- Giving examples.

- Checking out what others have said.

- Giving reactions to the contributions of others.

- Asking for reactions to one's own contributions.

- Initiating discussion by asking questions, giving ideas, making suggestions.

- Bringing together and summarising.

- Encouraging others to take part.

Figure 2

---

following class before the close of the initial meeting. If every member of the group is asked to undertake this work, including the tutor, this can underline the message of group as well as individual responsibility. It is important not to devalue this preparation by a rushed briefing. Rather, establishing a climate of serious academic intent can be reinforced by taking time to brief the students fully – for example, by pointing out how the preparation will be used in the next tutorial and by leaving space for students to ask questions. Having the details on paper also underlines the importance of the issue. These measures help to signal to the students the value that the tutor places on the contribution that everyone can make to the early work of the tutorial group.

Ground Rules

Ground rules are literally rules which the members of a group agree to have in place to guide their work. (For example 'students and tutor will arrive on time', 'sessions will not over-run at the end'...). Framing such rules can head off behaviour which might otherwise irritate some members of the group.

Involving students in agreeing ground rules has several advantages:

- students are immediately valued as having ideas of their own;

- the process involves everyone in modelling some of the working methods which may apply in the group (for example, proposing a ground rule means offering it for scrutiny and experiencing confirmation, qualification or rejection of it);

- tutors have an early opportunity to show how they will work in the class – for example, by chairing or passing over the management of the process entirely to the group.

Setting ground rules can most appropriately be done once students know the purposes of the tutorials and the responsibilities that they and the tutor have. Knowing the likely pattern of work in the group provides a practical context for thinking about appropriate rules.

Putting time aside for this process and involving the whole group can give a strong sense of ownership to ground rules. In turn, this can have a positive influence on the rules being honoured. If the agenda for the initial meeting is already overfull, agreeing ground rules is something that can be returned to at the following tutorial when students have had time to consider the matter more fully.

Once you become familiar with the place of your tutorial series in the course and the broad pattern of work for the term, you may wish to make an early start with drawing up a programme for the first meeting with your tutorial class.

- *What do you see as some of the essential items of business you will need to include?*

- *What activities might have a place in your programme to give students an early chance to participate?*

TUTORIAL PREPARATION

The Value of Preparation

Regular preparation by students and tutors can help the work of the tutorial class in a number of ways. Students who come well prepared are in a position to contribute. Moreover, material they bring will have received some prior thought. Taking part from such a platform can reinforce confidence and motivation for continued involvement in the group's work.

For tutors too, careful preparation can give a well grounded sense of security. Understanding the subject material means they can set tasks which really mesh with the learning aims. They will also be in a strong position to listen effectively to the exchanges of students during a class and to respond appropriately.

Potentially, these advantages of regular and effective preparation by students and tutor can significantly raise the quality of the work that a tutorial group will achieve.

Preparing the Students

Tutors can take a number of steps to help ensure student preparation is undertaken. Particularly during early classes, it can be useful to set tasks which are limited in scope and achievable. Initially, students are likely to be able to handle tasks which are fairly concrete in nature ('Read pages x to y then note three reasons why you think ...'). Being able to complete such preparation will quickly help students to develop confidence. Progressively more challenging work can then be given. This graded approach may help avoid the loss of student motivation which can happen if early preparation is too abstract and outstrips their skill levels.

Tutors can also encourage students by setting tasks on material which relates to core course content which will underline the central importance it has for their learning; also, indicating how prepared material will be used in the forthcoming tutorial can help motivation. Giving instructions in writing avoids confusion, saves valuable tutorial time and ensures they can be sent on to those who may be unavoidably absent. Finally, students are more likely to complete preparation where they have ready access to necessary source materials. Checking out resource availability and taking steps to resolve difficulties is an important part of setting preparation.

In addition to taking steps to encourage students to prepare for tutorials the quality of preparation is also an important consideration. Here there are a number of points to bear in mind.

Setting preparation in the form of questions acts as a stimulus to reflective thinking. This is much more valuable than unreflective reading. Setting sub-groups of students different preparatory tasks on a common subject can be an effective way of ensuring a wide and varied set of contributions without overloading any one student.

When preparation is set it is desirable that all students undertake it – otherwise, when the group meets, those who have not done it may be marginalised from the proceedings. This is a particular hazard when tutorials are structured round a student presentation of a paper or an essay. Often only the presenter and the tutor have a basis for discussion. If this approach is adopted, it is useful if the presenter involves the other members of the class in preparation – for example, by providing a synopsis of the talk plus a series of questions to trigger students' responses prior to the session.

Where classes are based on students' presentations, tutors can help speakers gain from the experience by directing them to advice about how to present a paper as part of their preparation.[3,4] Clearly this will be of particular importance where the development of communication skills is a high priority.

By thinking through student preparation in such ways, tutors show that they see it as a significant part of the tutorial group's work, that they are placing trust in the students to meet their responsibilities and that they are trying to ensure that tutorial sessions are grounded in students' own work.

> *Given your particular tutorial circumstances, what strategies do you think will be most effective in getting students to undertake preparation for your early classes?*

Preparation by the Tutor

In undertaking their own preparation, tutors will find it helpful to hold firmly in focus two perspectives. First, preparation needs to be to some degree flexible – a planning for possibilities rather than for a relatively rigid path as would be entailed in preparing to deliver a lecture. This is because the course a tutorial takes can be unpredictable – the unexpected can and does occasionally occur. For example, students may become absorbed in discussing a topic and what was envisaged to take ten minutes extends to half an hour. Alternatively, the tutor may expect students to find a particular conceptual area difficult but this turns out not to be the case and the group moves forward much more quickly than expected. Given such possibilities, tutors need to avoid being over rigid in their planning.

The second point relates to an important distinction in the way tutors approach preparation of their subject-matter for tutorials and preparation for one

particular aspect of managing the group. Preparation of subject matter lends itself to an incremental approach – for example week by week. But as group managers, tutors may have to respond to a range of commonly occurring situations, such as having some apprehensively silent students in the group, at any time. Becoming aware of strategies to deploy in such circumstances before tutoring begins is sensible so that the tutor can deploy them as and when the need arises. This aspect of tutor preparation is dealt with in *figure 4* opposite.

Tutorial Content

Figure 3 summarises the main steps involved in preparing a tutorial programme. In practice the process will often be a freer and more iterative one than the diagram suggests. It does however provide an organising framework to appreciate what is involved.

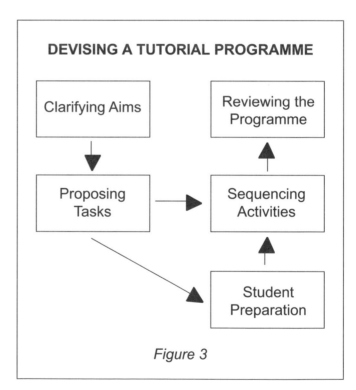

DEVISING A TUTORIAL PROGRAMME

Clarifying Aims

Proposing Tasks

Reviewing the Programme

Sequencing Activities

Student Preparation

Figure 3

The goal is to produce a coherent programme of learning tasks for the students to work with which will enable them to achieve the learning aims set for the session. Illustrative examples of learning tasks drawn from a wide range of disciplines show the enormous range of possibilities:

- translating a section of foreign language text;

- listing items from experience;

- identifying the form of a movement from a symphony;

- listing items culled from reading;

- solving a problem;

- discussing a presentation;

- devising categories for data or observations;

- giving reactions to/opinions about an exhibit;

- discussing critically;

- filling in the missing parts in a musical piece;

- generating ideas;

- arguing relative merits;

- ranking/rating/comparing values;

- drawing up a list of similarities and differences.

The range of possible tasks is limitless and devising them offers tutors considerable scope for providing creative learning opportunities for their students.[5]

As emphasised earlier, clarity of learning aims and a clear understanding of the subject matter which is the focus for the tutorial are fundamental. Tutors need to be sure that proposed learning tasks will address both of these. Some of the other variables against which tutors can usefully check a proposed task are:

- an estimate of how long the activity will take;

- whether the available room arrangements are suitable;

- availability of resource materials;

- whether it requires the tutor's involvement and if so, when and in what roles;

- whether the method it involves will assist the continued building of a supportive learning climate – for example activities which provide opportunities for individual work followed by sharing in pairs or threes are useful for this purpose;

- what briefing students will require and whether this needs to be put on paper beforehand.

Thinking these issues through will not only help a tutor decide whether a task is acceptable, but also where best it fits in the sequence for the class. In drawing up the final programme, the tasks the students have undertaken as preparation also need to be incorporated into the sequence. Finally, a check is needed to ensure that time has been set

---

DEALING WITH PROBLEMS

Some suggestions for dealing with five common problems are given below:[6]

Non-preparation by students. This can happen for a range of reasons despite tutors' best efforts. For example, students may have several courses and with heavy schedules may give preparation for a particular tutorial series a low priority. Tutors can anticipate this by having materials available relevant to the subject in hand – perhaps a few prepared questions or short readings – and commence with the students working on these. It is important that tutors do not reinforce non-preparation by giving summaries or solutions to the set work themselves.

Students who are hesitant about participating. The most constructive way to avoid having silent students is to provide tasks which begin with students thinking about an issue and logging their responses. Sharing these in pairs or threes is invariably successful in involving everyone. Grouping up into fours or sixes will provide confidence building opportunities for shy or nervous students to get used to speaking in front of larger numbers.

Students who dominate. Whilst students who make a surfeit of contributions may inhibit others, they are nevertheless precious assets and it is important not to alienate them. Putting dominating students into a common sub group will provide others with space to talk. Tutors can also lead from the front on a one-to-one question and answer basis to ensure everyone has opportunities to participate.

Dealing with the inaccurate. In some circumstances a blind eye to the occasional inaccuracy may be appropriate. Where a shy student, for example, summons up the courage to say something which is incorrect, ignoring the issue may be justified in the interests of encouraging more (accurate) contributions. Frequently drawing attention to inaccuracies risks both focusing the proceedings on the tutor and also the creation of a negative climate. These outcomes can be avoided to some extent if other students can be used to resolve some of the inaccuracies.

Handling difficult questions. Occasionally students will ask questions to which tutors do not have the answers. Conscientious tutors need not fear this situation and students will invariably welcome candour from the tutors about it. Putting the question back into the group can often produce an answer from another student. In the last resort, the tutor can give an undertaking to check the point before the next meeting.

Figure 4

---

aside for other necessities such as administration and setting of preparation for the next tutorial.

The end product of this process is a map of the tutorial session giving details of the activities the students are to undertake and an indication of what the tutor and students have to do.

It is easy to under- or over-estimate what can be achieved in a tutorial session. You may find it helpful to draw up an outline of a programme for an early class, thinking through each proposed activity against the above constraints – and any others which may apply. Reviewing your proposals with an experienced and trusted colleague can act as a useful check on their suitability.

CONDUCTING TUTORIALS

There is a great variety in the way that tutorials unfold in different subjects over the allotted time. Despite this variety in detail however, a general similarity of form is recognisable. Most classes move through three stages with particular functions associated with each (see *figure 5*). Broadly, an *opening phase* is followed by a *main working phase* which is succeeded by a *closing phase*. We will look at these stages in turn and the functions of the tutor in each, paying detailed attention to the activities of the main working period.

Opening Phase

This period is usually in the form of a tutor led briefing and is concerned with making clear to everyone the work to be undertaken, how it will be done and the various roles members of the class

will play. Typically it might include:

- a reminder of the aims of the session;

- an indication of how the work will connect to other parts of the course;

- a briefing about the activities to be undertaken;

- an indication of where and how students' preparation will fit in;

- guidance about the methods to be used and the specific ways everyone is expected to contribute;

- a reminder of any particular ground rules that apply.

Making such matters clear helps students see how their learning might develop in the session and can reinforce the sense of trust and openness in the group.

Main Working Phase

The form of the main working phase varies from the simple to the complex. At one extreme, an open group discussion embracing everyone may be the sole activity. At another, students may be involved in a series of sub-group activities and plenary sessions more akin to a workshop. Whatever the pattern, however, the tutor's essential functions are to manage the proceedings and to use their expertise so that students are able to make the most of the learning opportunities.

To see how tutors do this in practice, we will consider two contrasting situations where the full group is to work on a single activity. The first example is overtly tutor-led, in which the task involves, say, the translation of a foreign language text or a keyboard harmony exercise. The second example is of an open discussion, with the tutor's role akin to that of a chairperson.

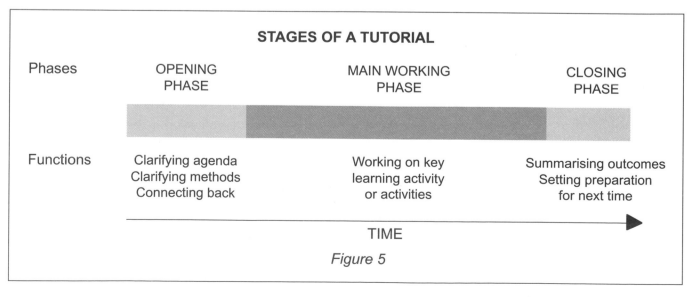

Figure 5

Starting Off the Activity. The initial goal is to draw the students into purposeful work. Invariably this means giving an introduction, preferably a short one to avoid the leadership of the session becoming anchored with the tutor. It could end, say, by directing students into the details of textual translation or by phrasing a suitable open question to get discussion underway ('What views do you have about ...?', 'What do you think of ...?'). The chances of students becoming involved will be increased, of course, if the tutor leads directly into their preparatory work. Especially in the opening few minutes of an activity, tutors need to be alert to the danger of reinforcing passive tendencies in the group by over responding to questions which cast them in the role of information providers. Where queries arise, tutors will assist the group's purpose if their replies are brief and they return the business to the students.

During the Activity. Once the activity is under way, the tutor's task becomes a three-fold one of:

- *attending* to what takes place, by observing and listening;

- *mapping* what is heard and observed on to the tutor's own knowledge and reflecting on it;

- *responding* to what is taking place with various strategies which may include questioning, commenting or taking other management action.

WHAT TUTORS DO IN TUTORIALS

ATTENDING TO *by listening and observing*	PROCESSING *by mapping onto own knowledge, reflecting*	RESPONDING TO *by questioning, commenting or management action*
Students' engagement with intellectual content of learning task	e.g. what is valid or invalid? - areas of misunderstanding? - degree of depth? - degree of breadth? - issues/areas well understood?	e.g. directing discussion by: - giving supportive feedback - switching the agenda focus - encouraging deeper or broader coverage - correcting misunderstandings
Students' demonstration of intellectual skills of the discipline	e.g. examples of skills being well used or underused: - reflection - analysis - synthesis - creativity - communication	e.g. feedback to students: - commending their use of particular skills - encouraging them to practice neglected skills
Patterns of students' contributions	e.g. dynamics of participation, espec. recognising: - who needs encouragement? - who needs constraining? - who/what is constructive/helpful?	e.g. judging when and how to: - invite in the quiet - restrain the dominant - reintegrate the whole group
Pattern of tutor's contributions	e.g. reviewing whether you are: - intervening too little? - intervening too much? - attending in a balanced way to all dimensions? (subject content/ subject skills/patterns of student contributions)	e.g. deciding to give the group: - more space - more trigger material - more feedback on their progress

Table 2

These activities apply to the students' engagement with the subject matter, the students' attempts to use their disciplinary specific intellectual skills, the patterns of interaction amongst the members of the group and the tutor's awareness of his/her own behaviour. Additionally, the tutor is carrying out these activities in a fluid group setting with considerable pressure to make immediate responses.

Table 2 shows the three elements of the tutor's task in relation to these four dimensions. Some illustrative examples of processing and responding activities are also shown. To illustrate what is involved in practice we can return to our two contrasting approaches. Typical patterns of interaction in a class during a translation activity or keyboard harmony exercise(A) and an open discussion (B) are shown in *figure 6*.

This brief review illustrates how all dimensions of the framework shown in *table 2* have a place in two widely contrasting situations. In any tutorial, needless to say, the emphasis given to the different

CONTRASTING PATTERNS OF TUTORIAL INTERACTION

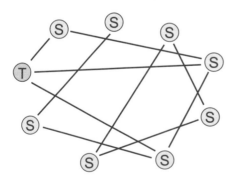

A. A CLOSE TRANSLATION OR A KEYBOARD HARMONY EXERCISE

In A, the tutor pays close attention to each student's understanding of the textual/harmonic content and also their proficiency in the skills of translation/playing. The need for managing the group may seem at first sight to have little prominence as the interactions are channelled through the tutor and the dominant exchanges are on a one-to-one basis. However, the tutor faces some subtle management decisions – for example in maintaining the involved interest of everyone in the work of the group whilst at any time only one student is speaking/playing; in deciding how long to keep the translation/score with any student; or when to progress to a weaker or a stronger student; and perhaps in deciding when to switch the whole group into open or structured discussion to review general issues which may be arising from the work. With the tutor controlling the pattern of students' involvement and also being the source of technical expertise, there are strong tendencies towards reinforcing student dependency to which the tutor needs to be constantly alert.

B. AN OPEN DISCUSSION

In B, there is much scope for a diversity of student opinion and argument to be expressed. The tutor's group management role is often prominent as students are encouraged to contribute. The degree to which the discussion is based on the ideas and views of students will also be influenced by how restrained the tutor is in promulgating his or her own.

Thus the tutor's self management and group management skills significantly influence the outcomes from discussion activity.

However, many students can be unsure about what they have achieved at the end of a discussion session. If they are to get a balanced picture of their achievements it is vital students receive feedback from the tutor about what they have made of the subject-matter and also about how they have gone about the work. Tutors are well placed, as chair or as an observer of a discussion, to do this. By monitoring the breadth and depth of discussion, they can prompt further exploration as required; by commenting on examples of students' use of skills they can encourage their further development.

To be effective, tutors need to identify the different strands that emerge during a discussion and to spot important themes that do not. Being able to remember who said what is also important so that contributions of individual students may be acknowledged and valued.

Figure 6

facets of the framework will be influenced by the learning activities being used and the personal style of the tutor.

How might new tutors best put the information contained in *table 2* to practical use? It is easy for new tutors to become overwhelmed by the complexity of all that happens in a group. Hopefully this information will help tutors appreciate that an order can be placed on events. It is clearly not possible to attend to all of these dimensions at once and even very experienced tutors occasionally find they are stretched by the demands. A helpful way forward may be to view the framework as something to be used selectively rather than a comprehensive map of what has to be attended to at all times. Thus, as the occasion and the mood suggests, tutors may in one part of a tutorial pay attention to the students' use of skills, and in another part, focus on the dynamics of what is going on in the group whilst all the time picking up on how well they are handling the subject material. Hence the tutor's task may seem more manageable.

Skills for Tutoring. The discussion so far has not addressed the particular skills which tutors can deploy in the *attending* and *responding* aspects of their work. There are many such skills and here attention is drawn to only a selection of them. Two skills of *attending* are picking up on *non-verbal cues* and *note-taking* and two valuable response skills are using *non-verbal signals* and *questioning tactics*.

Non-Verbal Cues. During a discussion, regular scanning of the tutorial group will enable tutors to pick up cues of facial expression and body language from those not speaking. From these, those who have something to say or those who are showing developing disinterest can be recognised.

Note Taking. In discussions ideas do not necessarily come out in a logical flow. Keeping a brief set of notes against a clock-face diagram can help to register who said what. This will enable a tutor to attribute ideas to those who produced them when giving feedback. It will also help to identify some of the key themes touched on when pulling together summary comments for the close of a session. Students need to be told about the tutors' purposes in keeping brief notes.

Using Non Verbal Signals. In discussion, responding to non-verbal cues with non-verbal gestures can be an effective way of keeping things moving without obtrusive verbal intervention. For example, tutors can bring in people or encourage them to continue by eye contact or hand gesture; or they can encourage them to stay out with a raised hand.

QUESTIONING STRATEGIES

Testing Questions

Used to elicit information and concerned with:

checking knowledge:

Which of the social indicators will be most reliable?

comprehension:

What do you think is meant by ...?

application:

What relevance would that have in ...?

analysis:

What qualities do they have in common?

synthesis:

Could you summarise what we have said so far?

evaluation:

What do you feel is best?

Clarifying Questions

Used to ensure a shared understanding (often by elaborating a point previously made):

What did you mean by ...?

Can you give an example ...?

Elaborating Questions

Often provide a gentle way of encouraging students to say something more fully - both about thoughts or feelings:

Can you tell me more about that?

What does that make you feel?

Implicit in the above are two *forms* of asking questions - open and closed. Closed questions usually offer little scope for response ("What was the date of the first NHS act?"). Because students risk answering wrongly, these may act to inhibit discussion. However, they clearly have their place where checking of factual material is required. Open questions, such as the examples of elaborating questions above, allow more scope for response. They will often draw students out and their use is a powerful enabling strategy in discussion work.

Figure 7

Questioning Strategies. In the course of tutorials tutors often wish to ask questions of their students.[7] Some common categories and purposes for which they may be used are given in *figure 7*.

A final point to make about using questions is that the quality of students' responses will be raised if they are given a short period of time to think before responding.

Closing the Activity. As was suggested earlier, there is often a need for the tutor to draw out from an activity what has been achieved. Quite apart from the value of reminding students about the ground covered, tutors can also use their greater awareness of the subject at this point to help round out students' understanding. They can show how the group's work connects into the wider picture or perhaps draw attention to areas which were under-explored and where some supplementary work may be needed. This process need take only a minute or two and it can be a very effective way of helping to consolidate students' learning. As the group gains in experience, students can be asked to provide summaries themselves.

Closing Phase

As just described, a principal purpose of the closing phase of a tutorial can be to look back and clarify what has been achieved. An equally important function is to look ahead and anticipate the work the class will handle next time by briefing the students about any preparation to be undertaken. Tutors often find that for a variety of reasons the ending of a tutorial becomes a rushed affair and the best laid plans go awry. In such situations, they can feel driven to cut short a review of the current session or trim the briefing for the next. Clearly, sometimes needs must, but the danger of giving students mixed messages is one tutors should keep in mind. Tutorials are important precisely because the students appear centre stage. Thus, reviewing what has been achieved and going over what has to be done for next time and making time to ensure these processes are considered ones, shows how much the tutor respects and values the efforts of students and continues to expect of them.

This chapter has focused on one of the major aspects of tutors' practice, the preparation for and the managing of students' learning in tutorial classes. Tutors make significant contributions to their students' development too through the guidance and support they give to coursework written assignments. This is the theme chapter 6.

Though few new tutors can be expected initially to have an array of finely tuned skills to manage a tutorial group, all tutors will be able to handle some aspects of this complex task well.

Which aspects of the framework shown in table 2 will particularly apply in your tutorial situation?

Which do you already feel some comfort with?

Which do you feel you might make an early focus for development?

FOOTNOTES AND REFERENCES

1. At certain points in this handbook (see also pp. 55-56, 62 and c.f. pp. 69ff.), we have used the term "academic discourse" to refer to the distinctive ways in which those within an academic discipline communicate with one another. This form of discourse involves much more than the use of technical terms or specialist jargon. It is characterised by distinctive ways of thinking: a concern with theories, concepts and abstract ideas; an alertness to the available evidence; and the grounding of discussion and debate within an established body of published scholarship and research. Needless to say, if students in higher education are to succeed academically, they have to master the language of academic discourse, as it is manifested in the particular disciplines or subjects they are studying.

2. Gibbs, G., Habeshaw, S. and Habeshaw, T. (1988). *53 Interesting Things to Do in Your Seminars and Tutorials.* Bristol: Technical and Educational Services, pp. 15-18.

3. Gibbs, G. (1992). *Discussion with More Students.* Oxford: Polytechnics and Colleges Funding Council, pp.31-34.

4. Race, P. (1992). *500 Tips for Students.* Oxford: Blackwell, pp. 45-47.

5. Jaques, D. (1991). *Learning in Groups.* London: Kogan Page. pp. 75-82.

6. Lublin, J. (1987). *Conducting Tutorials.* Kensington, New South Wales: Higher Education Research and Development Society of Australasia.

7. Jaques, D. Op.Cit. pp. 129-136

Chapter 4
Problem-Solving Classes
Derek Arthur

INTRODUCTION

In many important respects, tutorials in the sciences share similar characteristics to their counterparts in the humanities and social sciences. Across this spectrum of disciplines for example, tutorials provide an invaluable link between the concentrated delivery of material in lectures and students' private study, while also giving students opportunities to work interactively with their peers and with a tutor. Equally importantly, tutorials in all of these subject areas enable tutors to contribute their insights and understandings without denying students the chance to take responsibility for their own learning.

Yet there are also differences which sharply distinguish tutorial practices across the arts–science continuum. Perhaps the most fundamental of these differences stems from the nature of the course material. In mathematics, the natural sciences and engineering, the subject matter is characterised by strong logical threads, which in turn leads to a fairly strict sequential presentation. Students are exposed to a hierarchical structure or a series of stepping stones, where failure to understand one topic can prejudice their chances of coping adequately with later topics which build on it. Hence, an individual with a 'mental block' on a topic, especially one near the start of the course, can quickly land in a perilous state.

The present chapter focusses on tutorials of this kind, dealing particularly with *problem-solving* tutorials. The examples presented are drawn from mathematics, where, it can be argued, the purest form of problem-solving is to be found. As defined here, problem-solving is taken to mean any exercises set for students to solve. In mathematics these exercises are usually *objective* in nature. The problems are tackled by a *solution* method which is often either correct or incorrect and, if there is an

answer, it is often either right or wrong. This distinction is a crucial one: some problems, such as 'what is 2+2?', have an *answer*, while others, such as 'show that 2+2=4' have a *solution.* Furthermore, the working which leads to an answer is also treated as an integral part of the solution. In other forms of problem-solving, this is not necessarily the case. In data analysis or experimental design, for example, there may be no single correct solution but rather a spectrum of possible answers with some more valid than others. However, in both cases the objective nature of the subject matter strongly determines the content of problem-solving classes and the teaching approach followed.

The material in this chapter has been structured to guide new tutors as they pass from appointment, through training and preparation, to conducting regular problem-solving sessions with their groups. Tutors are invited:

- to review what is meant by problem-solving in the light of recent research;

- to reflect on their own abilities and assumptions about problem-solving;

- to acquaint themselves with the purposes tutorial sessions serve in their discipline;

- to consider in detail the way first and later sessions are prepared for and managed;

- to establish good practice in the marking of submitted coursework.

Throughout, an assumption is made that the tutor will be working in the context of a small group. Some courses may hold problem-solving classes with a large group of students in one room, with several tutors in attendance; much of what follows still applies, suitably scaled-up, but there is clearly little opportunity for group discussion where classes are very large.

PROBLEM-SOLVING

A great deal of research, principally by the artificial intelligence community, has been devoted to discovering how people solve problems and, as a corollary, to find methods to improve problem-solving skills. Much of this has involved mathematical problems, which avoid extraneous distractions, although some of the ideas which have evolved have been applied to other science disciplines. Indeed, certain of the phenomena have been detected in areas outside academia, such as the business environment. Some of the salient points are presented below, as a complement to chapter 8, *Student Learning* .

Prior to this work, the key categories in problem-solving were thought to be factual knowledge (resources) and methods for applying that knowledge (heuristics). The most influential contribution, by Schoenfeld[1], introduced two further categories, the strategy which guides use of resources and heuristics (control) and the solver's attitudes (belief). These four categories are expanded and illustrated in *figure 1*, and some further comments are made below.

Resources

The delivery of these is primarily the job of the course team, but the securing of them, and the eradication of 'bugs', i.e. systematic flaws in their use, are important responsibilities for tutors.

The course team will undoubtedly want students to develop a sound technique in standard problems, and will see private study, backed up by tutorial provision, as the best way to ensure it. There is evidence to support such an aim[2]. It appears that we have the ability to process information 'automatically'. Since students are often overwhelmed by the number of processes they need to control when tackling a novel problem, it helps when they can switch some processes to 'automatic'. A useful analogy is riding a bicycle. Learning to do this is a daunting task because of the number of different factors which must be controlled. An experienced rider does not have to think about balance or pedalling and can concentrate on steering, signalling, pacing, etc.

Although resources are clearly of critical importance, investigators have found students unable to solve problems for which they already possess the necessary resources and more! Scanlon[3] reports physics students who understand concepts but cannot solve problems involving them.

PROBLEM-SOLVING CATEGORIES

Resources

- knowledge about the problem domain
- facts, data and definitions
- ability to execute algorithmic procedures
- ability to carry out routine procedures
- knowledge of rules of discourse

Heuristics

- use an analogy
- draw a figure or graph
- try some special cases
- identify sub-goals
- try working backwards
- derive something from the data
- identify a related problem
- make use of symmetry

Control

- identify the key features of the problem
- consider all relevant methods before starting detailed work
- monitor solution process
- assess validity of intermediate solutions
- be prepared to switch method
- do not commence complicated analysis unless it is clearly unavoidable

Belief

- unquestioned intuitive knowledge, possibly incorrect
- use of a particular heuristic, such as a diagram, for every problem
- belief that solution is correct, even when palpably wrong
- decision that something is 'obvious' when, in fact, it is false
- 'I can never solve such problems'
- 'That sort of problem is always solved using this method'
- 'All these problems can be solved by a slick method'
- 'These problems are always harder than they appear'
- 'This material is of no practical use'

Figure 1

Heuristics

Following the publication of Polya's classic book, *How To Solve It*[4], it was thought that resources merely needed to be complemented by a full list of heuristics. The programme to identify and use these has proved disappointing because of the sheer number, especially when some have to be subcategorised; Schoenfeld[1] lists five problems, each of which needs a quite different application of the heuristic 'Try some special cases'.

By their nature, heuristics tend to apply across a range of individual courses and so are rarely taught formally. This places responsibility on tutors to help students construct and develop an effective armoury. Although they are undoubtedly very important, they cannot replace inadequate resources.

Control

The large number of useful heuristics highlights the problem of choosing the best strategy for a particular problem. Knowing a heuristic is not enough; the student must also know when to use it.

Even when students are presented with a set of well-defined methods, examinations often uncover uncertainty when the problems are mixed, even when they appeared to have no such difficulty during term-time, when the choice of method could be deduced from the context. Students need to think carefully about the best approach, not only to choose a feasible one, but to choose an efficient one. Having chosen a strategy, they must be prepared to switch to an alternative as soon as further progress seems impossible.

These so-called 'higher-order skills' – circumspection, monitoring and flexibility – are key features of successful problem-solving. Researchers have reported phenomena such as students considering candidate methods in the order in which they were taught[1] and apparently choosing a method on the grounds that it was the only one not yet used in that set of exercises[3]. Much research has been done by comparing experts and novices to see if the former can be role models for the latter. Silver[2] reports that experts tend to think qualitatively about problems before engaging in the detailed solution, while novices tend to start quantitative work immediately. A study in physics, where solvers were asked to identify key features of problems, showed that novices would give 'surface' answers, such as pulley, inclined plane, spring, while experts gave 'deep' answers, such as Newton's third law, conservation of energy. (The use of the terms 'deep' and 'surface' recalls work reported in chapter 8, and tutors will find several reflections of that dichotomy in the analysis reported here.)

Tutors must try to help students in this. Silver[2] remarks that textbooks, although excellent for presenting resources, are not good media for inculcating control.

> The demonstration and modeling needs to focus not only on *what* is being done but also on *why* the choice was made.

In tutorial work students should certainly be warned off an infeasible method, to save their time, but tutors ought to avoid telling a student directly the optimum method. Thinking about strategy may be part of the exercise, and hints, by means of a few carefully phrased questions, are more likely to preserve that. Entwistle[5] found students critical of very large problem-solving classes where they were unable to seek individual help. In these, students were shown the 'correct' solution, encouraging surface learning.

Belief

In some ways an unhelpful ingrained belief system is the most pernicious obstacle facing the novice problem-solver. Tutors must ensure they do not, by careless comments, further reduce the confidence of students who believe they are incapable of solving problems of the sort covered in the course. Also, they should bear in mind that, in spite of the initial aim of much of the research in this area, there is evidence[3] that experts may not be good role models, their performance being too 'opportunistic'. On a more positive note, they should encourage students to shed misconceptions about how problems are solved, about which method is 'always' best for a type of problem and about the usefulness of the material. It may be necessary to explain the need to ignore a 'world-view' when the material is counter-intuitive, as in some formal physics[1].

Thus, although intuition can be a powerful tool in determining a viable approach to a problem, it must not be applied unquestioningly. Encouragement to adopt the deeper approach discussed under 'Control', by stepping back from the problem and keeping an open mind about both the problem and the best strategy, ought to help develop students' skills.

Does Schoenfeld's analysis correspond to problem-solving as you see it in your discipline?

What mental processes do you use to solve problems?

Are there beliefs that you hold which may constrain your own problem-solving abilities?

Implications for Learning

The special nature of problem-solving leads to differences in the way tutorials are run, compared with those described in chapter 3. The principal ones may be summarised as follows:

- there is likely to be more individual or subgroup work and discussion, and less group discussion;

- there may be more emphasis on consolidation of the material than on extension, although this varies from course to course - this is especially likely in so-called 'service-teaching', where the course is a compulsory, but not mainstream, part of the students' curriculum;

- there will be more emphasis on logical and analytical thinking than on critical thinking;

- expression and argument are more likely to be expressed in writing;

- tutors may have less freedom to decide the content of classes – other staff may wish to tune the activity to the hierarchical structure they are building in their courses;

- there may be a wider range in students' ability to contribute to and gain from the tutorial session, although this may depend on the way students have been allocated to the different groups.

What then are the practicalities to attend to? What is it important to know about the day-to-day work of a tutor preparing to take problem-solving classes?

GROUNDWORK

It is often the case that tutorials form part of a teaching package. The basic course material will be designed and presented in lectures by a course team, headed by a course leader. Part of the responsibility of the latter is to ensure that tutorial staff are well-briefed about the course objectives and their part in achieving them. Tutors' contracts

should contain the name of the course leader for each relevant course, and tutors should feel prepared to approach that person if they require help or support.

Tutors who deal with problem-solving classes often have their duties prescribed in a fair amount of detail. There are three common ways in which they receive guidance about this.

Student Information

Tutors should be provided with the same information booklets or sheets as the students in the course. These should be studied in detail as they are likely to set out course aims and objectives, recommended textbooks, assessment information and other helpful organisational details. Indeed, it is not uncommon for tutors to be asked questions by their tutees which can be answered by reference to this! Care should be taken, however, not to stray beyond this, for example in responding to questions such as "Will I get an exemption from the examination?" which are a matter for the course leader.

Initial Briefing

It is usual for tutors to receive briefing before the course commences, concerning items such as the backgrounds of the students in the various groups, the method of marking coursework and perhaps even a preferred plan for tutorial sessions. This is best provided by means of a meeting of the course team and tutors, backed up by written instructions. If, through pressure of time, a meeting of all tutors proves impossible, course leaders will try to meet tutors individually, especially those new to the course. At this stage, tutors should ensure instructions cover foreseeable questions. This includes the problems which can arise in the delicate area of assessment of coursework where it is essential that all tutors adopt the same rules.

Regular Briefing

Tutors should receive instructions and suggestions for the material to be covered in each session. The more the course team desires to prescribe the work of the session, the more detailed this is likely to be. A specimen instruction sheet, for a mathematics course, is set out in *figure 2*. Such information should be helpful in showing what material is to be mastered, although probably less on how.

Note the portion at the foot of this sheet, which invites tutors to feed back information about the

SAMPLE TUTORS' ADVICE SHEET

Mathematics 2Eh

Tutorial Date: 22nd November

Material Covered in Lectures:

> The use of differentials to deal with implicit functions, particularly 'equations of state', such as those which arise in thermodynamics. (Note that this is less important for the groups which meet at 10am.) Determination of stationary points, mostly for functions of two variables, and their nature. Constrained problems, solved using Lagrange multipliers. The solution of the $\frac{\partial L}{\partial x_i} = 0$ equations for Lagrange multiplier problems is less important than learning how to define L and how to interpret the λ_i values.

Hand-in Questions:

> Worksheet 6; Exercises 12.4 and 13.2

Suggested Tutorial Work:

> The stationary point material is the most important. The theory is fairly straightforward, and students usually find more difficulty in manipulating the resulting equations. 13.1 and 13.5 are both standard problems and good for practice in solving the equations. 14.2 is a good constrained problem, since it is a compromise between being sufficiently general and being too complicated.

Solutions to be given to the group: 12.1-14.3

Next Week's Hand-in: Worksheet 7; Exercises 15.2 and 16.1

Tutor's Report Section

Students giving rise for concern (with reasons):

> Smith has now been missing for two weeks. Brown handed in very poor work, and has told me he is struggling in this topic. I gave him some pointers to help him back on the rails, but I fear he may need more direct help.

Students previously reported, now improving:

> Jones, who missed the previous two sessions, has now reappeared. He has been ill, and I gather his Director of Studies will contact the Department.

Other comments for Lecturing Staff:

> Most students found the solution of the Lagrange equations difficult, and would like some guidance on how important this is for examination purposes!

Tutor signature: F. Bloggs

Figure 2

students in the group and the course material. Tutors not invited to feed back information in this way should not, however, feel inhibited about conveying comments to their course leader.

Coursework – Early Thoughts

Throughout this chapter it is assumed that students will have submitted material for marking prior to the meeting of the group, and that it will be the duty of the tutor to return the material, and perhaps also to mark it. (If that is not the case, the reader may safely skip the parts below which cover coursework.) Although guidance on marking will be given at the end of the chapter, it is useful to address here the various reasons why course teams require coursework to be submitted, since it may affect the way tutorial sessions are run. There are several reasons, some or all of which may be relevant for a particular course:

- it encourages students to keep pace with material – if the material is structured hierarchically, it is particularly difficult to catch up and grasp new material at the same time;

- it can be diagnostic, helping students to assess their progress, tutors to assess where help is particularly needed and the course team to assess the success of the teaching;

- it may be instructional, for example using a problem the solution to which enhances the students' grasp of the subject;

- it often provides a contact point between the tutor and the group or even individual students - it can suggest where tutorial discussion should commence;

- it may contribute to the overall assessment.

These reasons indicate some very beneficial features of coursework as far as the tutor is concerned. Care must be taken, however, if there is an assessment role. The tutor should try to emphasise the positive aspects, and to relegate his or her role of allocating marks as merely acting as an agent of the course team, under its instructions. Fairness in marking and openness when questioned about decisions will help in this. Tutors who feel apprehensive about this are urged to seek early guidance and advice from experienced staff.

Looking ahead to your tutorial classes, can you identify any issues for which you would welcome clarification?

TAKING TUTORIAL CLASSES

The primary aim of the tutorial sessions is to encourage the development of students' capacities to apply material more formally delivered in other components of the course, and to extend their studies to fresh material, albeit based on what has already been presented. This is implemented by giving each member of the class access to a person of appropriate academic standing. This is in marked contrast to lectures, where the objective is essentially to deliver fresh material to the students, and the amount of contact between lecturer and individual class members is minimal. Because the tutorial is a timetabled point of contact between staff and students, great importance is attached to its success.

The content of this chapter is based on the premise that the tutor's role is not only to be a source of academic expertise but also to encourage members of the group to seek and draw on that expertise. In order to give encouragement, however, the tutor must attempt to develop a suitable atmosphere in the tutorial. The tutor should aim to be perceived by the group as a 'friendly guide', who is interested in the welfare of his or her tutees (primarily their academic welfare, but also more than this if it helps the working relationship without unduly burdening the tutor); who is keen for members of the group to be successful academically and who is seen to be keen in this way; who will go to considerable lengths to sort out the difficulties presented to him or her by the tutees, and will also attempt to communicate his or her own enthusiasm for the subject to the tutorial group. Nonetheless, it is advisable to avoid undue camaraderie, lest the tutor becomes unable to maintain 'ground rules' (see later) such as prompt arrival and timely submission of coursework.

In trying to achieve such an atmosphere, there are a number of practical steps which the tutor can take (detailed in later sections); equally, in dealing with the minute-by-minute cut and thrust of a session, the tutor has to rely on a combination of experience and intuition for which it is difficult to formulate rules other than to try to adhere to the general principles presented here.

As explained above, there is likely to be more emphasis on individual than on group teaching. The group size is likely to represent a compromise between the desire to make it as small as possible, thereby maximising contact between tutor and individual students, and the resources available. The conduct of a 'small' group, say with 12 or less students, will depend on the attitude of each participating person, the students no less than the tutor.

We make an implicit assumption that the tutor will stay with a group for a significant period. Some courses have a more fragmented structure; also, on occasion a tutor may have to act as a 'stand-in'. In such instances course leaders have to develop long-term plans and tutors can help them by briefing those who will take over when they have completed their own stint.

Content of Session

Course Objectives. Some courses may have very concrete objectives, such as achieving the ability to solve specific problems. The problems set are likely to be those with a specific answer. Students will not necessarily judge that the style and presentation of the solution are as important as the correctness of the answer! Tutorial help is then likely to revolve round the abilities of individuals to achieve the objectives. This situation is most common in 'service' courses, such as mathematics courses for engineers and scientists.

On the other hand, some courses may have more open-ended objectives, such as achieving an understanding of some body of knowledge. The problems set may require the student to demonstrate the truth of a result, with the style of argument and its lay-out being of great importance. Here there is more scope for discussion, with the tutor helping elucidate key features and possibly links with other material. This situation tends to occur in courses where students intend to proceed to Honours in the discipline, particularly in the later years of the course when they have gained in confidence.

Group Profile. Students may be allocated to groups according to one or more of the following factors:

- home department (for 'service' courses);

- background (H-grade, CSYS, A-level);

- demonstrated ability (grade in school examination, performance in previous university course);

- different learning types - see chapter 8, *Student Learning* – such a classification is currently rare, largely because of the difficulty in implementing it.

Whether or not such allocations are good practice, they may be impossible to achieve for various reasons; tutors must then be prepared for an inhomogeneous group, which may present delicate problems in balancing time. It is recommended that tutors ask the course leader about the group background if such information has not been divulged.

Coursework. As explained in the next section, most courses set work to be done privately and handed in for comment and possibly assessment. Where marking is undertaken by the tutor, the work is usually returned in the tutorial session, which clearly affects the running of the session. There is a delicate issue here; coursework is an invaluable diagnostic instrument for both student and tutor, yet there is an obvious danger that the tutor's role may be undermined if he or she is regarded primarily as an 'assessor'. If any grades allocated

```
POSSIBLE ACTIVITIES

• review of coursework

• tutor-led discussion

• student-led discussion

• worked example (by tutor)

• worked example (by student)

• group work

• individual work (solo)

• individual work (in group)

Figure 3
```

are to count towards the overall course assessment, tutors should strive to be tactful in any comments made, whether spoken or in writing. (Some advice on written comments is given towards the end of the chapter.)

We have already mentioned that there are few general rules for what must be contained in a specific session. Some possible activities for the session are set out in *figure 3*. These will be discussed in more detail later. The decision as to which of these to employ at any time may be determined by numerous factors, such as prescription by the course team, student choice, tutor suggestion and the course of events within the session.

Preparing Students

It is important to stress the need for students to prepare for each session. Tutors should set an example by being well-prepared and aware of the context of the tutorial and the learning aims associated with it.

Students ought to have been told that the success of tutorials depends on their willingness to contribute to the proceedings, and that success in this is largely achieved through preparation before the tutorial, which will inevitably identify difficulties, and thus generate points of query for the student to bring up at the tutorial.

In practice, there is usually variation in the willingness of students to do adequate preparation or to contribute to the tutorial. It is a further aim, for which the tutor is largely responsible, to encourage preparation by showing how it improves the success of the session.

To this end, tutors could consider suggesting problems to be tackled before the session, unless that is already done by members of the course team. Such problems should be fairly straightforward to ensure students are not discouraged; after all, they will be tackling them without tutor help.

It is sensible to make it clear to the group that it can only function as a coherent unit if everyone does the same preparation, which is another reason for setting tractable problems. If some special activity is planned, such as a student presentation, then the entire group should be briefed; a suitable hand-out could be prepared in advance.

Recall that the session interfaces both with the lectures and the students' private study, which indicates two main aims – providing back-up for material formally delivered to the class as a whole and helping students' individual attempts to come to terms with that material. Their preparation should enable them to benefit from help in both directions.

Tutorial sessions are also effective in engendering a spirit of group-work, even if that is not an explicit course objective. If students can achieve fruitful collaborative work in a problem-solving class, there is a good chance that they will continue to work in that way for a proportion of their private study time. Provided there is true collaboration, this is an effective and efficient method of developing problem-solving skills.

> *Detailed aims for tutorial sessions are strongly influenced by the discipline, both in what knowledge and abilities students are expected to gain, and in the way they are to work towards gaining them. A similar statement can be made about the sort of preparation which students should carry out.*
>
> *Given the particular tutorial circumstances you expect, what strategies do you think will prove most effective in encouraging students to undertake preparation?*

THE FIRST SESSION

It is now time to consider activities in the actual sessions. We start with some thoughts about the very first session, which will provide the tutor with some idea of the background and aspirations of the students, as well as providing an opportunity to mould the working of the group for future sessions. It hardly needs to be stated that the first meeting of the group is of key importance - first impressions can be difficult to change!

Getting to Know the Group

This should be the first activity. Mastering names and faces as quickly as possible is both efficient and effective. The course team may help, for example by asking students to produce passport-sized photographs. One possibility is to ask each student to announce their name, their reasons for taking the course and any other background information that might be helpful. This has the bonus of ensuring that every member of the group contributes at the outset, and also ensures that the students in the group get to know each other. Once introductions have been made, it is good policy to address students by their first, or given, names; after all, that is how they will address each other. How students should address the tutor can be agreed between those involved.

It is important to remember, too, that some individuals will find problem-solving difficult and may require to work slowly and steadily, with only rare flashes of inspiration. Such students may well be taking the course by compulsion rather than choice, and some may initially feel resentment. The tutor will often start out with an advantage in not being one of those who selects and delivers the material in the first place, and so is not associated with their discomfort. It is hence particularly important not to undermine that advantage by careless comments, forceful behaviour or demonstrations of easy brilliance, most especially at the outset.

Ground Rules

These are rules which all members of the group should accept in order to facilitate smooth running of the sessions. If the tutor's first session is at the start of the course, it is worth discussing with the group such rules and also their preferences for how the session should be run; it is good policy to review this at a later session. If the tutor is taking over mid-course, however, there is much to be gained by consulting the previous tutor (if possible) about the working of the group. Tutors should show from the outset that they are willing to be guided by reasonable requests.

In the case of first-year courses, students will usually be encountering tutorial sessions for the first time since leaving school, and the tutor may need to take a lead by suggesting enough basic rules and procedures to get the sessions off the ground. These can then be adapted and added to as the students gain more confidence. How to establish and maintain observation of ground rules, in general, is well-covered in chapter 3.

> *Can you think of additional ways in which you could help students get to know each other better?*
>
> *Looking ahead to your tutorial classes, which 'ground rules' would you like the groups to consider adopting?*

REGULAR SESSIONS

It is usual for the tutor's contract to specify that proper preparation must be carried out prior to the session. Otherwise it would be impossible to make good use of a period of, say, 50 minutes. We thus start with consideration of this vital matter, before discussing how its results are put into use during the class.

Tutor Preparation

The first step is to consult the course team's instructions and then study the material for the session, ensuring a reasonable degree of comfort with it. There may well be copies of guidance notes (as in *figure 2*) or model solutions to help in this. If there remains a problem, consultation of one of the set texts (mentioned in the course information sheets) may clear it up.

It is particularly important to pay attention to the context within which the material is presented. There are several factors to be considered:

- the depth of student knowledge;

- the sequencing of concepts - in pure mathematics, for example, it is possible either to define concept A and then prove result B, or to define concept B and then prove result A;

- any specialisation or simplification assumed by the lecturer concerned;

- which particular methods are advocated for solving a problem;

- notational or layout conventions;

- any possible relationship with material in students' other courses - this is particularly useful in 'service' courses, where it may help motivate the students and clarify the problem through discussing it in a familiar context.

Once the material and its context have been assimilated, any coursework should be 'marked' and commented on, as discussed later.

It is now time to prepare a programme for the session. There may be matters left over from the previous session to supply an opening line; alternatively, marking coursework may have suggested matters to be covered.

Flexibility is a key feature of any plan. Students may ask for a different topic to be covered; some new issue might arise in the process of dealing with the planned one; some material thought to be difficult may turn out to have been more easily grasped by the group. A careful consideration of time management is necessary, especially if faced with different demands from various members; 50 minutes for, say, ten individuals suggests a delicate balance must be struck between individual and group activity.

Finally, there are various potentially tricky situations which can arise in individual groups. Since these usually require careful handling they are explored in some detail in chapter 3.

> *It is difficult to estimate what can be achieved in the time allotted for a group whose characteristics you do not yet know. Try drawing up an outline plan for what you think may be a representative session. It may also be helpful to discuss this with a colleague who has previous tutoring experience.*

Activities

Figure 3 set out some activities which could form part of a typical session: these are now expanded in the subsections below. Note that these are only indicative of what is possible; the list is neither complete nor compulsory. Further suggestions are offered by Hubbard[6].

Taking Attendance. If this is a requirement for the course, it can be done in conjunction with returning the coursework. In early sessions it can be made to appear part of the name-learning exercise. A middle course is to be steered; students should be aware that it is being done, but equally it should not be seen to be a big issue. If it is queried, it can be pointed out that attendance is a course requirement (probably set out in the course information sheet). It could even be added that it is a deliberate attempt to put a little pressure on students to attend, and so maintain an interest in the course, as experience normally shows a close correlation between those who fail to attend and those who fail the course!

Outlining Plan for Session. A brief outline should be given leaving, indeed encouraging, members of the group to comment. The plan should be updated in the light of replies.

Distributing Marked Work. Tutors should be careful not to use up time unduly in this way by labouring points already marked on the work; it is better to allow students to query written explanations they cannot follow. For some courses, the timetable can dictate a considerable time lag between the delivery of the material and the return of the coursework associated with it. In that case the course will have moved on to new material, and students should be coming to terms with the next assignment. Problems experienced by individuals should have been flagged on the scripts themselves. If remedial action is needed for most of the group, that should be included in the plan for the remainder of the session. The distribution of work is a useful activity for the very start of the session, since it does not compromise those who insist on flouting the 'ground rules' by late arrival.

Working on the Board. Tutor work on the board should normally be minimal, otherwise the tutorial becomes a lecture and the potential advantages of group work sessions are lost. The most useful role for the board is when there is a need to explain a point to the majority of students in the tutorial. Typical circumstances are:

- nearly everyone is baffled by some point in the set work (if this is a major problem, it probably affects all groups, and requires remedial action by the course team)

- in the tutorial someone raises a point which, when put to the group, is of interest to nearly everyone

- there is an opportunity to improvise something for the whole class (see below).

When a tutor does work on the board, it is good policy to ask the group questions, to see if they can fill in some of the points. This should avoid the students switching off on the grounds that the session has become another lecture. Sufficient time must be left for 'thinking', to avoid undue dependence on the tutor. It is important, however, to avoid embarrassing silences; if no-one replies, the tutor may have to provide the answer or perhaps start again with some further hints and suggestions. Tutors should not feel unduly apprehensive about this, since ability to judge when to intervene should develop with acquaintance with the students.

Grouping Students. This may be an effective way of getting students to help each other while the tutor is occupied elsewhere. One possibility is to arrange three students round a table or set of desks, with the tutor dropping in from time to time to fill the vacant slot. Some tutors like to carry a supply of triplicate paper, so that a copy of any written illustrations can be left with each student. Hubbard[6] discusses in detail various ways of grouping students.

In mathematics courses, some students may wish to work singly. It should be possible to allow both styles in a single tutorial, at least at the start of the course. Arranging small groups helps students get better acquainted. The use of such groups, however, must be carefully monitored. It is important to avoid the development of 'freeloaders' who take advantage of others' preparation. A group will work more effectively if all students have undertaken similar preparation; that can be used as a basis for allocation.

Students sitting side-by-side or in groups should be positively encouraged to discuss relevant points with one another. Sometimes their discussions may stray rather a long way from the tutorial topic, in which case a discreet reminder of the ground rules is called for. However, from the point of view of good atmosphere, it is probably sensible to allow a little 'social' conversation, but this needs to be kept within fairly tight limits.

Spreading Attention. If the group is working in subgroups, the tutor's attention is likely to be focussed on just part of the group or possibly one individual. At such times the rest of the tutorial group should be busy. To ensure this, early in the tutorial, perhaps after any overall business is dealt with, it is necessary to make sure that everyone has something to work on. The lecturer may have suggested a particular problem, but as different students are likely to have reached different places on the sheets, it may not be advisable to be overly prescriptive about the work set for the tutorial hour. Any tutees currently unattended should be encouraged to call the tutor over if they encounter difficulties. If a point raised by a tutee looks interesting, he or she could be asked if it could be put to the whole group. If so, and it appears to be of wide-scale interest, do it on the board or, better still, get one of the group to try it.

Student Board Work. With some groups it may be possible to encourage a member to work on the board, which is an excellent exercise for all concerned. If a student is willing to respond to this, but then does something incorrectly, he or she should be let down gently. The tutor should try to find something positive in what has been done, but suggest that there was a point which had been overlooked; thanks should be expressed for the effort. If the work done by the student is correct, then praise is in order!

An alternative strategy is to ask the students at the board to act as a 'scribe' only. This takes much of the pressure off that student while forcing the others to communicate their contributions with clarity and precision.

It is, of course, necessary to take a great deal of care in choosing suitable topics for such work. Students are likely to resent it unless they have been given time for preparation. It would also be a mistake to involve only one or two students from the group. Whether or not to make regular use of this activity will depend on the students' backgrounds and abilities. It is likely to be inappropriate in a 'service' course or in a 'weak' group if students have been allocated by means of previous record. Suitable topics include:

- an exercise from the problem sheets or textbook

- an interesting point which has arisen in the group and could be 'researched' before the next meeting

- an investigation related to the course material

- a summary of the week's work from a student viewpoint.

Improvisation and Participation. Much of the best teaching that is done is improvised; it has a spontaneity that may be missing from formal lectures. If, before or during the tutorial, an idea appears which is relevant to the course (not necessarily all that directly: a different viewpoint, an overview, a neat method, a biographical detail,

an interesting application, etc.) which can be put across without excessively labouring the point either on the board or verbally, it is worth seizing a suitable opportunity to air it. These excursions from the more routine work add precisely those bits of colour that will communicate enthusiasm for the subject to students. If some audience participation can be included, perhaps through selective questions, so much the better.

Tutors should not worry unduly if some technical device doesn't work when improvising. It is perfectly reasonable for tutors to be honest – admitting that the step eludes them, and promising to sort it out in the quiet of their own room; they must, however, make sure they do, in case the same question comes up the following week! Occasionally, students ask really searching questions, and if the answer can't be found immediately, this should be admitted with a promise to find out. It does students no harm to see that tutors are fallible, in fact it may well encourage them.

Winding up. It is good policy to summarise the session, feeding back any useful points which have arisen. If possible, pointers should be given for next week's preparation, this being a good way to encourage students to prepare for the sessions, in order to get the most out of them. This does depend on the course team briefing tutors on what is likely to be covered in the intervening period.

This is also a good time for the tutor to have a quiet word with any students who appear to need further help, directing them to course leader, lecturer or any drop-in consultancy service. Chapter 7, *Supporting and Advising Students*, gives further advice on this.

After the session has ended, tutors should complete any feedback sheet for the course team. They should report on any illnesses, either a retrospective report by the student, or a rumour from others in the group, as well as recording any student whose progress causes concern. Indeed, the type of information sheet exemplified in *figure 2*, if used, requires this.

Though few new tutors can be expected initially to have a wide range of finely tuned skills, all tutors will be able to handle some aspects of this complex task well.

Think through the various activities reviewed above. Are there any which you feel you will need to investigate in more depth? If so, you could consult an academic colleague or some of the books on tutoring[7].

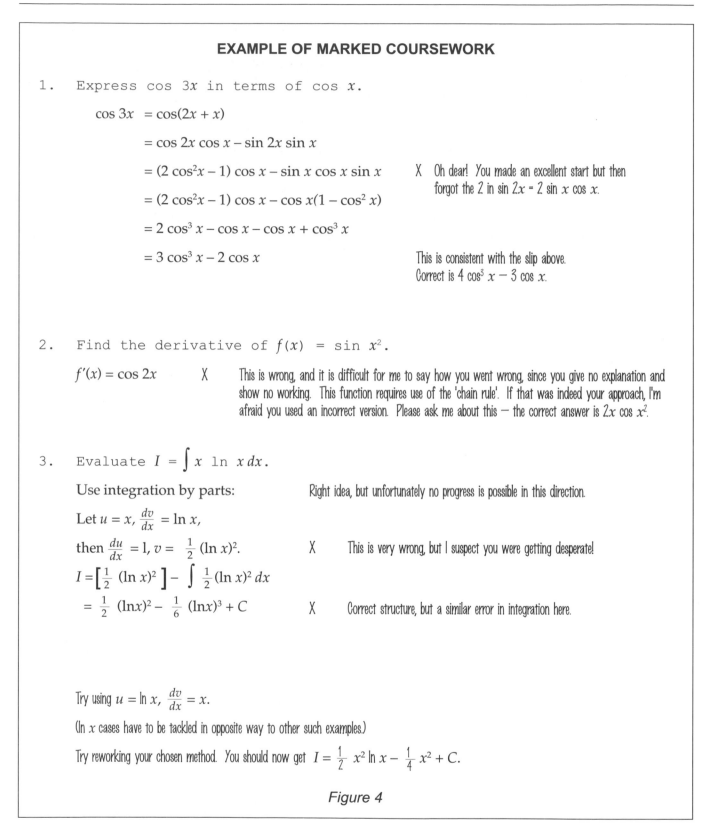

EXAMPLE OF MARKED COURSEWORK

1. Express cos 3x in terms of cos x.

$$\cos 3x = \cos(2x + x)$$
$$= \cos 2x \cos x - \sin 2x \sin x$$
$$= (2\cos^2 x - 1)\cos x - \sin x \cos x \sin x \qquad \text{X} \quad \text{Oh dear! You made an excellent start but then forgot the 2 in } \sin 2x = 2 \sin x \cos x.$$
$$= (2\cos^2 x - 1)\cos x - \cos x(1 - \cos^2 x)$$
$$= 2\cos^3 x - \cos x - \cos x + \cos^3 x$$
$$= 3\cos^3 x - 2\cos x \qquad \qquad \text{This is consistent with the slip above.}$$
$$\text{Correct is } 4\cos^3 x - 3\cos x.$$

2. Find the derivative of $f(x) = \sin x^2$.

$$f'(x) = \cos 2x \qquad \text{X} \qquad \text{This is wrong, and it is difficult for me to say how you went wrong, since you give no explanation and show no working. This function requires use of the 'chain rule'. If that was indeed your approach, I'm afraid you used an incorrect version. Please ask me about this — the correct answer is } 2x \cos x^2.$$

3. Evaluate $I = \int x \ln x \, dx$.

Use integration by parts: Right idea, but unfortunately no progress is possible in this direction.

Let $u = x, \frac{dv}{dx} = \ln x,$

then $\frac{du}{dx} = 1, v = \frac{1}{2}(\ln x)^2.$ X This is very wrong, but I suspect you were getting desperate!

$$I = \left[\frac{1}{2}(\ln x)^2 \right] - \int \frac{1}{2}(\ln x)^2 \, dx$$
$$= \frac{1}{2}(\ln x)^2 - \frac{1}{6}(\ln x)^3 + C \qquad \text{X} \qquad \text{Correct structure, but a similar error in integration here.}$$

Try using $u = \ln x, \frac{dv}{dx} = x.$

(ln x cases have to be tackled in opposite way to other such examples.)

Try reworking your chosen method. You should now get $I = \frac{1}{2} x^2 \ln x - \frac{1}{4} x^2 + C.$

Figure 4

MARKING AND FEEDBACK

In what follows it is assumed that the main objectives in having work handed in for 'marking' are to provide diagnostic feedback and immediate help. Assessment towards the overall performance is assumed to be incidental to the tutor's role.

It has already been noted that problem-solving exercises tend to have an objective solution or a set of particularly creditable solutions. Students who have encountered difficulties with the tasks set may place 'blame' on the members of the course team who set the exercises and decided the mark scheme. This is an important observation, since it enables tutors to preserve their relationship with the students, even if assessment is involved. To maintain good relations, tutors should strive to put over the positive side of marking coursework, backing this up with tactful and helpful comments on the script.

Comments such as 'rubbish' should be avoided; it is better to use phrases such as 'no real progress here'. Students should be encouraged by writing comments such as 'good work' or (if a serious error creeps in) 'right approach'. It is worth considering phrases such as 'Oh dear, you've gone off the rails here' or 'Pity, you had made a good start' to indicate the tutor is as disappointed as the student by the error made. Friendly phrases help encourage students to submit work and, even if it really is 'rubbish', it is better to receive something than nothing; otherwise tutorial help cannot be fine-tuned to the student's difficulties.

If a student shows a serious misunderstanding, even

if the answer is nearly correct, adding 'Ask me about this' provides a starting point for tutorial help and discussion. References to course material such as printed notes or a set book, may be helpful to the student, but references to texts which are difficult to locate should be avoided, since that may waste students' time and result in lowered motivation. *Figure 4* provides an illustration of some of these points for mathematical coursework.

There are various common problems in dealing with coursework and these may be anticipated by the course team with specific advice. It is worthwhile thinking this matter through at an early stage, and tutors who are concerned by it should raise it at the briefing meeting with the course team. *Figure 5* draws together some potential tricky situations, with appropriate suggestions.

DEALING WITH TRICKY SITUATIONS

Poor presentation. The course team should provide advice about what is expected from the students, since their work ought to reflect the aims and objectives of the course. Matters such as the quality of layout and argument, will depend on the nature of the course - less emphasis on style and more on accuracy is common in 'service' courses. If such matters are important, tutors could perhaps comment separately and very briefly on coverage of technical points, presentation and logical argument. Again, a written comment such as 'Presentation - please ask' is liable to lead to a response in the tutorial where the tutor can elaborate.

Failure to complete parts of the assignment. Tutors should avoid simply spelling out a full solution, since that largely removes the point of the exercise. Instead they could try giving some broad hints, or even an outline of various key steps, followed by the final answer, if there is one.

'Cries for help'. Students may hand in blank or partially blank pages. In some cases this is a temporary problem caused by illness or finding that week's work particularly difficult. Help may be given as in the previous paragraph. In addition, it is important to enquire, tactfully, about the reason; if it was due to illness, the course leader may be able to excuse the student or to authorise late submission, if the grade is important. If, however, blank sheets or failure to hand in work is a regular problem, the student

will need encouragement. Some suggestions for handling this are given in the next paragraph.

Late Work. Some students stop handing in work because they have dropped behind. Under these circumstances, tutors ought to be willing to accept from the student work covered earlier in the term, to look over it and credit it in much the same way as the set work. (It may be that the marks cannot count, if specimen solutions have been issued; on the whole it is better to accept it and sort out the grading issue later.) Tutors should stress to such students that when they stop handing in work, it becomes impossible to gauge progress or to give appropriate help. Slipping behind puts their studies into a risky situation, and they should take active steps to catch up as quickly as possible. Such students should be given constructive advice, even if it is only to seek help from their personal tutor or the course leader.

Cheating and Plagiarism. These are very delicate issues. There is often a fine line between collaborative work and copying. Students can often fail to attribute use of other peoples' work through carelessness rather than deception. Where to draw a line may depend on the course aims, and the only advice possible, from outside the context of the course, is to consult the course leader. It is quite likely that the course team will have anticipated the situation and issued guidelines as to what is acceptable and what action to take if there is prima facie evidence that they have been broken.

Figure 5

If marks are to be awarded, tutors must ensure they 'follow-through' from errors to see if subsequent work is accurate. They should not be petty – obvious slips of the pen should rarely be penalised. If an answer appears to be correct, but there is doubt about the method, tutors can add 'benefit of doubt' to ensure the student is aware of that and can seek advice if, indeed, he or she was uncertain about the method.

Even if the assessment counts for a great deal, this need not undermine teaching aspects. The above advice remains valid, but tutors may need to give more written explanation on how marks were awarded, to show fairness and retain the students' trust. Examples are:

- 'Two errors here', when an incorrect answer has incurred a double penalty

- 'This error has made the rest of the question trivial', when the tutor appears not to have given as many marks as 'following-through' would indicate

- 'I was prepared to ignore this first time, but I must penalise you now', when a student repeats an error which may have been a careless slip had it occurred once only.

Do you feel comfortable about the level of detail you should give in response to missing or wholly inaccurate coursework assignments? If not, you could consult a colleague with previous tutoring experience in your discipline.

CONCLUSION

The task of tutoring in a problem-solving environment is a significant and stimulating challenge. To diagnose students' difficulties, and to help overcome them, often requires the tutor to replicate their thought processes. Each student's mind is unique, and the successful tutor will develop a battery of techniques to use on the diversity of issues which arise. The material in this chapter undoubtedly covers only a proportion of successful tutoring strategies.

REFERENCES

1. Schoenfeld, A. (1985). *Mathematical Problem-Solving.* Orlando, Florida: Academic Press.

2. Silver, E. (1987). Foundations of Cognitive Theory and Research for Mathematics Problem-Solving Instruction. in Schoenfeld, A. *Cognitive Science and Mathematics Education.* New Jersey: Lawrence Erlbaum Associates. pp. 33-60.

3. Scanlon, E. (1993). Solving the problem of physics problem-solving. *International Journal of Mathematical Education in Science and Technology,* 24, 349-358.

4. Polya, G. (1957). *How To Solve It,* 2nd edn. New Jersey: Princeton University Press.

5. Entwistle, N., Hounsell, D., Macaulay, C., Situnayke, G. and Tait, H. (1989). *The Performance of Electrical Engineering Students in Scottish Higher Education.* University of Edinburgh: Department of Education and Centre for Teaching, Learning and Assessment.

6. Hubbard, R. (1991). *53 Interesting Ways to Teach Mathematics.* Bristol: Technical and Educational Services.

7. Gibbs, G. , Habeshaw, S. and Habeshaw, T. (1988). *53 Interesting Things to Do in Your Seminars and Tutorials.* Bristol: Technical and Educational Services.

Chapter 5
Demonstrating
Iain Allison

INTRODUCTION

The development of students' skills of enquiry through practical and field classes is characteristic of a wide range of subjects, most notably in the physical and biological sciences, in engineering, and in some of the social sciences. Traditionally such practicals provide settings in which students can come to see how knowledge within a subject has been derived from experiment and application, whilst examining the interconnections between theory and practice. At the same time, while deepening understanding of the scientific method as it applies in their subject, students develop the organisational, manipulative and observational skills which are part and parcel of the conduct of experiments, projects and practicals. Last but by no means least these practical activities also help to inculcate appropriate professional attitudes.

Postgraduate demonstrators are not of course solely responsible for what and how students learn in these laboratory and field classes, since they are part of a team whose various members also include lecturers, tutors and technicians. Whether in the laboratory or the field, however, demonstrators tend to be in the front line of teaching and learning: it is with them that the majority of students are likely to have the most direct contact during practical work. And since most demonstrators will be closer in age to undergraduates than the more established members of the teaching staff, students tend to see them as closer to their own culture and hence easier to approach. Indeed, as a familiar presence, ready and able to lend their assistance, demonstrators guide students through the various stages of setting up, working through, recording and analysing the results of experiments, field trials and surveys. Their potential impact on the quality of students' learning is therefore profound. They can, for example, help students broaden their range of practical skills, encourage them to tackle problems

and difficulties confidently and clear-sightedly, and prompt them towards a firmer and more rounded understanding of the subject-matter of the course.

For the demonstrator too, the experience of teaching practical classes brings tangible benefits. Through their teaching, they too can enhance their understanding of their subject, while simultaneously developing the teaching skills of communication, support and guidance as they attend to those students who need their assistance. These are valuable transferable skills relevant to a wide range of employment opportunities both within and outside higher education.

This chapter focuses on practical ways of helping demonstrators approach their task with confidence. The chapter begins with an outline of the purposes laboratory and field classes serve. Next it reviews the principal aspects of the demonstrator's role: preparation; what is involved in running a practical class (including how to ensure the demonstrator's expertise can best be used to benefit student learning) and other tasks demonstrators may be asked to undertake such as the marking of field or laboratory reports. The special responsibilities involved in running field classes are outlined and a number of common concerns that demonstrators have to handle are reviewed. Throughout, appropriate cross references are made to other chapters in the handbook which contain material of value to demonstrators as well as tutors.

> *You have succeeded academically as a student and now, as a demonstrator, you can help others to succeed. Cast your mind back to the demonstrators who assisted in your undergraduate practicals: which of these stood out for you as particularly effective – and what was it, do you think, that made them so effective?*

Aims of Practicals

Learning aims are statements of general intent which indicate to students and teachers alike the general direction of the learning that is to be achieved in a course or part of a course. Thus, the general aim for practical classes is to enhance students' understanding of methods of scientific enquiry. This is pursued in a variety of well-established ways: for example, by giving students opportunities to undertake experiments, tackle problem-solving exercises, and carry out survey and project work, so that they can experience at first hand how the theory and principles of a discipline are applied. Yet while this general aim underpins virtually all undergraduate learning in the laboratory and in the field, it contains within it a number of more focused learning aims. These are summarised in *figure 1*.

KEY LEARNING AIMS IN PRACTICALS

- Consolidating subject knowledge;

- Introducing discipline-specific methods and procedures;

- Developing technical skills;

- Enhancing cognitive skills;

- Promoting teamwork skills;

- Increasing motivation.

Collectively, pursuit of these aims helps students appreciate both the method of scientific enquiry and professional attitudes appropriate to a given subject.

Figure 1

Consolidating Subject Knowledge

Consolidation is crucial since scientific knowledge in general and in most specific disciplines can be highly complex and abstract. Illustrating principles through concrete or simplified examples can be very helpful to students in illuminating core subject matter. Consolidating students' knowledge may be achieved for example by: illustrating material taught in lectures; simulating conditions in research and development laboratories; developing skills in communicating technical concepts and solutions; teaching theoretical material not included in lectures.

Introducing Disciplinary Methods and Procedures

Giving hands-on experience helps students appreciate the methods and ethos of practitioners in a discipline and thus contributes to the shaping of professional attitudes. Ways in which this may be done include: providing motivation to acquire specific knowledge; stimulating independent thinking; maintaining and deepening interest in the subject; teaching the principles of experimental work in the subject; showing the use of labs as a process of discovery.

Developing Technical Skills

Laboratory and field classes can provide frequent opportunities for students to learn how to use scientific equipment. This enables students to develop their technical, observational and motor skills, for example by: familiarising students with apparatus and measurement techniques; teaching basic practical skills; training students in observation; training students in keeping a day-to-day laboratory diary; training students in writing reports on experiments.

Developing Cognitive Skills

Carrying out experiments and projects can promote a range of cognitive skills involved in problem formulation and analysis, in classifying data, and in explaining results and predicting responses. Enhancing cognitive skills can be achieved for example by: training students in aspects of experimental design; teaching students to make deductions from measurements and to interpret experimental data; developing skills in problem solving; using experimental data to solve specific problems; fostering critical awareness by avoiding systematic errors.

Promoting Teamwork Skills

Practical exercises and experiments are often conducted in groups, where students can learn collaboratively. This method of working can lead to an appreciation of the value of working with others and insight into the skills needed for doing this effectively. Cooperative activities which can help to promote students' teamwork skills include: designing experiments; setting up experimental equipment; checking observations; sharing of possible interpretations from results; compiling group reports.

Increasing Motivation

The exchange of ideas inherent in working with other students can lead to a greater motivation towards and interest in the subject.

Demonstrators will normally be provided with statements of the particular learning aims of the courses on which they teach. It is essential that they become familiar with these – and especially the ones that apply directly to practicals – if they are to be in a position to offer focused and constructive support to students. For example, weak students may fail to see the particular point of an exercise they are undertaking, and the demonstrator can clarify this for them. Moreover, since practical tasks often contribute to a number of aims simultaneously, it can be useful for a demonstrator to be in a position to help students see the full range of ways in which a given exercise is potentially helpful. For example, during a field work survey students could be developing the specific technical skills of measurement and observation, whilst also learning how to work effectively in a group setting.

> *Take one practical course on which you will teach; looking through the list of aims above, which do you think will be most important for your course?*

Against this essential backdrop of learning aims, we can now turn to consideration of what is involved for the demonstrator in preparing for and conducting classes in the laboratory or in the field.

GROUNDWORK

Learning Objectives and Tasks

Within any given practical or field exercise, the students' learning is usually focused on a particular objective or outcome. *Figure 2* shows one example for a particular practical class.

The learning objectives, set and specified for each session, relate to the wider, overall learning aims for a course or a term. As a demonstrator, it is essential that you have a clear understanding of the learning objectives for each session so that these can be communicated to the students and the activities for the class (see for example *figure 3*) can be appropriately planned and pursued. Many of the skills learned during activities related to such objectives are transferable between disciplines. It is therefore helpful to point out to students that the skills they are developing in their practical work will be invaluable regardless of the discipline they finally specialise in.

It is important nevertheless that students fulfil the particular objectives set for them, and thorough planning and preparation can help to ensure that both students and staff leave the class at the end of the session with a sense of a job well done. You should therefore make the most of opportunities to

---

INSTRUCTIONS FOR A SINGLE CONCEPT EXPERIMENT[1]

Using a Cathode Ray Oscilloscope

The objectives of this experiment are to make you familiar with the controls of a simple cathode ray oscilloscope (CRO) so that you will be able to:

    i   Adjust a CRO to obtain a stable picture of an input waveform.

    ii Predict the effect of changing any one of the controls.

    iii Make measurements of the voltage and period of an input periodic waveform.

All these to be done using a Telequipment S51E cathode ray oscilloscope.

The cathode ray oscilloscope is probably the most used single piece of equipment in any scientific laboratory. Many different types and makes will be met during your course throughout the University. This experiment uses one of the simplest CROs available so that you may become familiar with its controls before passing on to more complicated types.

The programmed script includes an explanation of the function and operating principles of the CRO and takes you through the setting up and use of the instrument stage by stage.

Figure 2

TYPICAL INVESTIGATIONS UNDERTAKEN BY FIRST-YEAR STUDENTS IN AN INVESTIGATION LABORATORY IN BIOLOGY[2]

- How many bacteria exist in pasteurized and unpasteurized milk samples of different ages?

- How does temperature affect the growth of a yeast population?

- Can the alcohol content of fermented honey be increased by adding various mineral salts during fermentation?

- How effective are mouthwashes in killing bacteria in the mouth?

- What is the level of sewage pollution in Logan Creek as measured by fecal coliform populations?

- In what kinds of fruit juices do yeast cells grow best?

- What are the effects of household disinfectants on bacteria?

Figure 3

---

attend pre-class briefings where the learning objectives, content, level and potential pitfalls are discussed.

Your Role in the Teaching Process

This last point is a timely reminder that you will not be working in isolation: you are part of a teaching team which will encompass a wide range of experience, and which can therefore help you with various aspects of practical work. The team needs to work at working together, and needless to say, communication between everyone involved is vital. You will each have different roles to play and tasks to do, so make sure that you know who is doing what - communicate, don't duplicate. Precise responsibilities will however vary from one department to another and even from class to class. You may wish to consult with the course leader or your mentor if you have one, to find out about established ways of working in the department. Ensure that you know what the staff member in charge expects of you. Introduce yourself to the laboratory technical staff and find out about laboratory procedures.

The demands made on you as a demonstrator may vary considerably. At one extreme you may be present to assist students and answer queries without having been involved with the setting up of the practical; you may have neither continuity from one practical to another nor a longer-term commitment. At the other end of the spectrum you may be in sole charge of a group of students, ensuring that all equipment is available and working as well as being responsible for marking assessed work and giving written and oral feedback to students in your group. Some demonstrators

may be responsible for the provision of equipment and ensuring that technical staff are present to run it. Other responsibilities may include the distribution of handouts, the supply of consumables prior to the practical classes, and the distribution to students of specimen answers.

As a demonstrator you are one of the most valuable resources available to students, but they may need advice and in some cases encouragement if they are to gain maximum benefit from their interactions with you. Conveying what your expectations are of a class (and what your role in the session will be) can go a long way to avoiding misunderstandings or frustrations. It also helps if you keep in mind the wider context of a particular practical or set of practicals, so that you can forge links into the lectures and tutorials which go to make up the course.

Perhaps now is a good moment to review how clear you are about your role in the course team. On what aspects of that role would you welcome further information and guidance?

THE PRACTICAL OR FIELD CLASS

Preparation

Attending briefing meetings, familiarising yourself with laboratory or other practical settings and reading all the course documentation are sound starting points for any practical or field demonstrating. Once this has been done, organising equipment and the students' activities can then be your priority. If you are in charge of the practical class or field trip you must ensure that any necessary equipment is in place and working and that, for example, the necessary reagents are available. Ideally, you should have done the experiment or exercise so that you are aware of its specific demands. In any event, before the class, you should spend time working through the instructions and trying to anticipate where problems are likely to arise. Drawing up a plan for each session will also give you confidence to approach the task and organise the various stages. This will often involve thinking through each stage and reviewing what you want the students to have achieved, how long it is likely to take them and what will be required of you. This helps to get a good impression of how to deploy the time available for the class to greatest effect. It should of course be an objective that all students complete the work set, though in some cases this may not be feasible.

Students understandably expect clear guidelines on what is required of them and your verbal instructions should be backed up with a detailed written explanation of the work to be done. If this is not already in the laboratory guide or course book, you may find it worthwhile to add a handout of your own, or some other resource materials such as OHPs, slides, or video clips. Students will also expect you to have the answers to their queries and in the majority of instances it should not be necessary for you to have to check with the lecturer in charge. You are the expert in their eyes and if you constantly have to refer to higher authority it will undermine their confidence in you, while making untoward calls on the lecturer's time.

If reports have to be written or questions answered and handed in, then again clear guidance needs to be given about what is expected and you may need to check with the course leader what the precise requirements are for the course on which you are demonstrating. In early classes with any group some general tips on how to write laboratory or field reports will be welcomed along with more specific advice on adhering to discipline-specific conventions. In some cases, groups of students may have to deliver a presentation of their findings and you will therefore need to give thought to how they can best prepare.

Lastly, it may be advisable to check with the course leader about any individual students who may need to be given special attention because of, for example, specific learning difficulties, lack of attendance, poor laboratory reports, or problems in others areas of their work.

Safety

As a research student part of your initial training will have covered aspects of safety appropriate to your work and some of this may be relevant to your practical or field classes. It will rarely suffice to assume that, since safety regulations for conduct and good practice in laboratories are written down, the students will have read them; you must reiterate the main points and bring to their attention any specific hazards in each practical, including for instance vitally important regulations regarding clothing, eye protection, proper use of equipment, etc. Prior to the practical you should also check that the fire doors are unlocked, unless they are external alarmed ones. You should know where the nearest first-aid box is and where to find the nearest first-aider.

Your department may be able to pay for you to take an intensive training course on safety and health and this will add another valuable skill to your list of accomplishments. If appropriate you should have read the regulations on the Control of Substances Hazardous to Health (COSHH) and know the procedures to be followed in the event of an accident. The students will look to you to respond calmly but firmly, so think through what you would do if a particular accident did happen. Be familiar with the 'house rules' and, if eating and drinking are not permitted at laboratory benches, you should set a good example yourself and practise what you preach.

The Practical Itself

Figure 4 lists the things you should attend to or keep in mind during the class itself.

The desirability of taking a pro-active stance is worth highlighting; do not wait until a hand goes up seeking assistance but, rather, as you walk round the class, check how the quieter students are getting on. It is not always easy, however, to gauge the level of advice to offer; some students may not have studied the subject before and may therefore need a generous helping hand, while others may have a Higher-grade or A-level in it and need only a modicum of assistance in order to make further progress. In any event, you should never be standing around idly gazing out of a window or, worse, chatting with another demonstrator. That will convey the impression that you are uninvolved or even uninterested in how the students are getting on. Instead, you should systematically walk round the class checking on the progress of individual

---

THE PRACTICAL CLASS

Demonstrators should:

- arrive on time;

- liaise closely with the technician(s) and any other support staff;

- check and help with the setting-up of the equipment, specimens, etc.

- take attendance if that is required;

- start the practical with clear instructions to the whole group on learning objectives, the planned activities, the procedures for clearing up, and any issues of safety which particularly need to be drawn to their attention;

- give clear guidelines about any work to be handed in or assessed;

- allow time for questions at the outset to clear up misunderstandings;

- monitor student progress and respond quickly to raised hands;

- deal with problems arising;

- be pro-active: try to anticipate problems and deal with little local difficulties before they grow into larger and wider ones;

- keep your own notes of who has done what – especially important if there are several experiments or activities happening at once;

- sum up at the end – or better still invite students to collaborate in summing up;

- set follow-up tasks if appropriate, e.g. reading or preparation for next time;

- ensure students leave the laboratory or field in good order and equipment safe.

Figure 4

---

into spending excessive time on any one student or small group. If a student is having great difficulty which requires you to spend longer than, say, five minutes, it is time to take stock. Can other students help out, for example? Failing all else the student should be referred to the lecturer or supervisor; time-consuming remedial teaching is not part of your remit.

Though you should avoid being cast in the role of PC Plod, patrolling your beat and out to spot troublemakers, you can play supportive watchdog by keeping an eye on students' work and by asking questions as you walk around. Closed questions such as 'Doing fine, are you?' invites the non-committal 'yes' because a student may be reluctant to admit to being stuck or not understanding something. Open questions require longer answers and lead you into a more meaningful exchange which will allow you to gauge the level of understanding. Say, for example,

> I see you have the correct answer for this part, well done; now, how do you think you might tackle the next section?

Be sensitive too about body language: for example, a student avoiding eye contact may not only be unsure of how to proceed but may also have low self-confidence, and the challenge open to you is to assess the optimum level of assistance needed to help the student make headway without him or her feeling stupid.

With uncommunicative students it may be very difficult to assess their level of understanding and to motivate them without a two-way dialogue. Who looks puzzled? Who is bored? Or who has finished? Those who finish the allotted work early should be discouraged from leaving. Giving them more advanced exercises to work on will prevent the 'flocking' effect where the remaining students rush through their work in order to rejoin the growing 'flock' who have left early.

In some practical classes group work is encouraged and you may be called over by one individual in a group rather than by the group as a whole. Beware, therefore, of disrupting the group by speaking only to the one student, with the result that the others feel left out.

Similarly, if students are working more or less independently and one is having a problem, find out first if his or her neighbours are at the same stage and facing the same problem and encourage them to discuss it as a group. The skilful demonstrator will aim to draw out the answer from the students, and thus set them a challenge. Simply

students, offering a few words of encouragement or praise and keeping an eye open for small errors in, for example, the use of technical jargon or physical units and untidy work. Naturally you will be called over by individual students but you should try to ensure that you see how every student is progressing and that you do not miss anyone. A corollary is that you should be wary of being drawn telling them the correct answer will discourage them from trying to resolve difficulties by themselves.

Some of the questions students raise can be easily answered. At other times, the question may not be clearly formulated, and you will need to probe and perhaps back-track to a point where you are sure of the student's understanding and then lead on from there. The student may be feeling nervous and unaware that you may also be anxious about your ability to help. You can initiate a conversation with:

This looks very good, what are you going to do next?

or,

Did you see what happened when you . . . How do you explain that?

Once you have started a dialogue, things will run more smoothly and you can then focus more sharply on the subject matter. Sometimes a question is not really a question at all, but rather a plea from a student who just does not know where to start. In this case you should help the student firstly to formulate an appropriate question and then to try and answer it. Keen students who are actively involved with their subject are usually willing to tell you what they are doing. Here your task is easier but you still need to assess their understanding and to help them with the more technical matters.

Summing-up

It is invariably helpful for the class to conclude with a brief review or summing up and you will need to allow enough time for this. Take some time before and during the practical to jot down the points you wish to see drawn out. You may wish to draw a diagram or write a complicated equation on the blackboard beforehand so that you are sure you have got it right. And while you are giving explanations of points, remember to talk to the class and not the board. If students are struggling to understand, an explanation that is confusing and disjointed will only make matters worse. Drawing things to a conclusion and highlighting principles self-evidently aids understanding. It is also worthwhile to make sure that the links between the practical work and the theory have been made explicit: if appropriate, go over the exercise with the class while talking through it so that the students have an opportunity to watch how an expert goes about it. If appropriate, you could point out any follow-up reading or additional work that could be done.

FIELD CLASSES

Field classes offer various advantages and these are summarised in *figure 5*.

HOW DO STUDENTS BENEFIT FROM FIELDWORK?[3]

Students can gain the following advantages from field classes:

- They can observe first hand, or actually experience some of the phenomena of their subject. These might otherwise remain merely as 'stories' in texts. Who really knows what a chalk down is who has never walked on one?

- Students can obtain a real life experience of the realities of certain industrial, professional or environmental problems. Erosion is a physical fact that you can go and see for yourself. And when you have tried surveying, you have more respect for map makers.

- Related but distinct, is the hands-on experience of how hard it sometimes is to do well at some professional practice. How many species can you really put a name to? And, even if you do like looking at aerial photographs, can you take them yourself, even when you are feeling airsick?

- They can see the difference between the controlled variables of laboratory physiology and the irreducibly complex situation in the field.

- Students get a chance to think of questions they might otherwise not think of. I could not have asked the question I posed about 4th century Roman pottery, unless I had been present when it was unearthed.

- Finally, there is the matter of going there – and being there – the education gained from going to a place new to you, and being obliged to give it your most careful attention.

Figure 5

However, field classes do pose some special problems which include:

- safety - including the particular requirements that might be posed when the class takes place in difficult terrain or at a complex installation or plant involving hazardous processes;

- equipment - operation and safety;

- transport and logistics;

- student's disabilities or medical conditions - which will involve making sure beforehand that you are well-briefed about any such students in your group.

Any or all of these may call for rather more preparation than would be the case for a routine laboratory practical.

If students are given a pre-excursion briefing, be sure that you attend and obtain any documentation that is relevant. Indeed, if staff are conducting a pre-visit to the locality the demonstrators should be included. Safety is very important and appropriate clothing must be worn with specialist equipment where necessary; for example, hard hats for quarry visits. The students are not constrained within the four walls of a laboratory and one role of the demonstrator is to act as sheep-dog to ensure the party sticks together. Regular head counts may be necessary and often, with the lecturer concentrating on the science or engineering aspects, the responsibility falls to the demonstrators. If much walking is involved the party can easily get strung out and it is important to ensure that those at the rear do not miss out on any explanations.

Freedom from the laboratory may express itself in freedom to take liberties and start larking about. This must be handled carefully but firmly to avoid any incident getting out of hand and becoming a threat to the safety of the party. All the rules of the laboratory should pertain to excursions whether on buses or in the field.

Excursions often involve a greater degree of informality. In what ways could you capitalise on this to achieve high quality learning and encourage collaboration within and between groups.

POTENTIALLY TRICKY SITUATIONS

The practical exercise fails or goes wrong. Resist the urge to panic if things go wrong; it happens to everyone and you can no doubt recall mishaps when you were a student. Try to explore with a group or student why things have failed; check instructions have been followed; have you forgotten to mention a crucial point?; find out if it is an isolated incident or whether others are having trouble. If there is a problem with the whole class then the staff member in charge should be called in to review the situation. It could even be an opportunity to engage in some problem solving. If the equipment has broken down or failed you should call in the technician and not try to mend it yourself. In the meantime the students affected could join with another group, if appropriate.

A student is not pulling his/her weight in a group. Talk to the whole group about what they are working on. Try to involve everyone in the discussion and ask the less-than-involved students for their views and to outline their part in the proceedings. It may be necessary to allocate changed tasks within the group to engage the student with the work. Make a personal note that the students may have to be regrouped next session, if the problem persists.

Arguments between students. It is best not to get drawn into such arguments; rather be alert to the possibilities of tensions developing and move swiftly to defuse things. Focusing on the task in hand rather than on the dispute and trying to get the students to re-engage with the material with comments to encourage or direct them should help.

Disruptive students. This is likely to happen only rarely, but if it does you must move quickly and firmly to deal with the situation. Students who have given up because the task is too difficult, or because they have finished early and are restless, or for any other reason may become disruptive. Peer pressure is powerful and a single disruptive student may distract a number of others. There may be laboratory rules regarding conferring, moving around, etc. to prevent any particular student's behaviour becoming a problem and a swift reminder of these should be all that is necessary. However, if it is not, then it is the responsibility of the staff member on duty to sort it out. If safety is compromised then you must clearly act straight away to stop the student's behaviour. The safety of the whole class is of prime importance and if necessary the disruptive student should be required to leave and the staff in charge told.

An accident occurs. Think through in the planning stages for a session what you would do if an accident happens, whether in the laboratory or a field class. It is better to have thought this through rather than having to react on impulse, and you will be alert to possible hazards for each exercise. Students will expect you to know what to do. In the section on safety above, the importance of knowing the COSHH procedures was stressed. You have to deal with an accident straightaway and call in the first-aider if necessary and/or evacuate the laboratory. All accidents need to be recorded in the accident book and this is probably held with the technician.

Figure 6

Potentially Tricky Situations

You should take care not to be so engrossed in one group's problems that you lose sight of what is going on in the rest of the class. Remember that you are responsible for everyone and regularly keep a watchful eye on the whole group. *Figure 6* contains some potentially tricky situations with suggestions of what you might do.

ASSESSMENT

Reports of laboratory or field work have a well-defined structure and it is part of their training that students must develop the craft of writing their reports to conform with what professionals in their discipline expect.

If you are involved with assessing the students' reports from laboratory or field classes, chapter 6

LABORATORY REPORT ATTACHMENT SHEET[4]				
Name	Marker			
Date in	Date back		Mark	
Student's specific requests for feedback				
Marker's general view of the work				
Rating scale	*Excellent*	*Good enough*	*Not good enough yet*	*Comments*
Title and headings				
Summary				
Introduction: Importance				
Background				
Objective(s)				
Apparatus				
Procedure				
Theory				
Results: Presentation				
Accuracy				
Discussion				
Conclusions				
English: Sentence construction				
Spelling				
Clarity				
Tables				
Figures				

Overall assessment

Areas for improvement

1.

2.

Figure 7

LAB BRIEFING AND ASSESSMENT SHEET[5]

Lab ....

Student ....

Section	Briefing	Max. Mark	Your Mark	Feedback
Introduction Background				
Methodology Use of equipment				
Results Data analysis				
Discussion Conclusion				

Figure 8

Marking and Commenting on Essays may be read for more detail. You will need to get together with the teaching staff and other demonstrators to ensure that a consistent approach to marking is being followed. You will need to be clear in your own mind what the criteria are for what is an acceptable answer and what is not.

In many cases, a student assessment and feedback sheet of the kind shown in *figures 7* and *8* is used. And if you have some discretion over how you mark and comment on students' lab or field reports, you may like to consider using these examples as they stand, or in an appropriately modified form. 'Attachment sheets' or pro-formas of this kind can help you achieve consistency, while giving students well-focused feedback on the strengths and weaknesses of their written work.

CONCLUDING COMMENTS

In the light of the preceding discussion, it hardly needs saying that the role of the demonstrator is a challenging one. And while demonstrators generally have much less discretion over what and how they teach than do many tutors, the demonstrator's responsibilities, as we have seen, are no less exacting. Practical and field classes are usually much longer than tutorials, are often organisationally more complex, and are more critically reliant on the use of specialised equipment, facilities and materials. They also normally involve much larger numbers of students, all of whom will be looking to the demonstrator for information, expertise and guidance, deftly and sensitively given. Only very rarely, however, will a new demonstrator find that he or she can rise to this array of challenges with effortless ease. As with any other demanding professional role, success will come not just from being well-prepared but also from taking stock: what aspects of the role are being done well, and which need more attention? Chapter 10, *Feedback on Teaching*, outlines various ways in which you can periodically review your effectiveness – and indeed relish the many tangible contributions you can make to your students' learning. As a Bristol University student once observed:[6]

> The demonstrator usually manages to find something you aren't clear on and quiz you about it, so that by the end, you do get a little bit more understanding about it.

It is often in such small triumphs as this, steadily accumulating from practical to practical, that the greatest rewards of the demonstrating role are to be found.

REFERENCES

1. Boud, D., Dunn, J. and Hegarty-Hazel, E. (1986). Teaching in Laboratories. Milton Keynes: SRHE & Open University Press. p.38.

2. Boud, D., Dunn, J. and Hegarty-Hazel, E. op. cit., p. 46.

3. Horobin, R., Anderson, B. and Williams, M. (1992). Active Learning in Practical Classes. Effective Learning in Higher Education Module 6. Sheffield: CVCP. Part 1, pp. 37-38.

4. Brown, S., Rust, C. and Gibbs, G. (1994). Strategies for Diversifying Assessment in Higher Education. Oxford: OCSD, Oxford Brookes University. p. 39.

5. Gibbs, G. and Jaques, D. (1990). Labs and Practicals. Oxford: OCSD, Oxford Brookes University. p. 40

6. Boud, D., Dunn, J. and Hegarty-Hazel, E. op. cit., p. 77.

Chapter 6

Marking and Commenting on Essays

Dai Hounsell

INTRODUCTION

As a tutor, you may well be asked to mark and comment on at least some of the essays and other written work which your students submit as part of their coursework assessment. This chapter is therefore concerned with what is involved in marking essays accurately and reliably, and in providing students with constructive feedback in the form of written or oral comments.

At base, assessment entails making an informed and considered judgement about the quality of a student's performance on a given assignment. Coursework assignments require students to 'put their learning on display',[1] so that tutors can evaluate:

- how well the subject-matter has been grasped;

- how effectively students have practised the critical and analytical techniques which that discipline calls for – whether it be English Literature, Physics, Economics or Anthropology;

- students' degree of mastery of the skills involved in communicating ideas and evidence clearly and cogently.

Needless to say, evaluating essays and other coursework assignments is a crucial as well as a demanding task. Tutors have a responsibility to their university and to their chosen discipline to ensure that appropriate standards are pursued and upheld. Equally, they have a responsibility to their students, whose academic progression depends on the grades they receive, to mark their work fairly, consistently and promptly.

Yet assessment, it needs to be emphasised, has not one main purpose but two: coursework enables university teachers to judge what standards students have attained, but it also provides students with the feedback they need to learn effectively. Even the earliest research efforts by psychologists, nearly a century ago, established the importance of what was then called the Law of Effect: it is hard to make headway in any kind of learning task if you do not have a firm impression of how well you are doing.[2] Feedback on coursework meets this need by alerting students to their strengths and to their weaknesses, and by suggesting how the quality of their work might be improved. Feedback therefore helps students to focus their intellectual energies in the most productive way, and thus to achieve the best of which they are capable. And in so doing, it makes it possible for universities to set and to sustain high academic standards.

This chapter explores how you might best pursue these twin purposes of coursework assessment – what we might call *assessment-for-grading* and *assessment-for-learning*. It looks at what you will need to do to prepare the ground, for yourself and your students, prior to a coursework essay; at what marking and commenting on students' work will involve; and at what is likely to be required to ensure that your marks and comments are taken note of and followed up. First, however, it looks at what is known about how students go about their coursework and what they derive from it. The majority of the findings discussed originate in studies of undergraduate essay-writing, although many of these findings are applicable to other kinds of coursework assignments.

> *As a tutor, you are obviously someone who has done very well academically - so well, perhaps, that it is easy to lose sight of what a typical undergraduate student can realistically achieve. You might therefore find it helpful at this point to try and think back to your early (and perhaps faltering and uncertain?) experiences of what writing an essay was like in your first year at university. And if you still have your first-year essays on file, why not take a look at them again with a fresh eye, to jog your memory?*

COURSEWORK AND STUDENT LEARNING

"I sit at my window" says a character in Jean Rhys' *Wide Sargasso Sea*, "and the words fly past me like birds – with God's help I catch some".[3] Writing seldom comes easily to most people. It is a struggle to commit one's thoughts, ideas and feelings to paper in a way which seems to do them justice.

For most students, too, writing takes very considerable effort. It also occupies a large swathe of their independent study time. In some universities, arts and social sciences students are required to write the equivalent of one essay every ten days; and even where the volume of coursework is not as high as this, writing assignments is nonetheless time-consuming. Some students, it seems, manage to get their essays written in under ten hours; others may take as long as thirty, extending over several days or even weeks.[4] Equally pertinently, students and tutors alike are inclined to underestimate just how much time is required to complete a coursework assignment.

One well-designed Australian survey looked at a large variety of assignments across a wide range of subject areas, and compared tutors' and students' forecasts of how long it would take to write each assignment with the time students actually spent. On average, the students spent nearly twice as much time as they had anticipated – and almost *three* times as much as their tutors had estimated.

Given what preparing and drafting an assignment involves, however, the amount of time and effort required is hardly surprising. First, coursework is typically stipulative: it is the teacher rather than the student who decides what the topic is to be, how it is to be tackled, what counts as 'essential' or recommended reading, and how long the finished assignment should be. Students therefore have to work closely to this brief, rather than being free to follow their own instincts or preferences. Second, assignment-writing involves an intricate series of steps, as shown in *figure 1*. It is worthwhile taking a closer look at these six steps. We can explore the demands which each step makes of students and begin to reflect on what implications this might have for the guidance students will find most helpful (a question to which we return later in the chapter).

Choosing a Question or Topic

A student's usual first step is to choose the essay topic or question to be tackled. Having several different titles to choose from is not necessarily liberating, as the following comment suggests:

> It's horrible when there's about eight choices, 'cos I'm like a rabbit, a rat with several traps – I don't know which one to stick my head in.

Some students, of course, put off deciding which title they will tackle until they have done enough of the required reading to be able to make a more informed choice. And as class sizes rise at a time when library budgets too are under pressure, it is important to bear in mind that students' scope to choose between assignment topics may be more apparent than real. Which topic is eventually chosen may be influenced as much by the availability of library copies of recommended reading as by what most engages a student's interest.

Analysing the Question or Topic

Assignment titles and topics are usually crafted with great care. Most university teachers take pains to devise titles which will subtly stretch students' intellects whilst at the same time focusing their energies within realistic and manageable bounds.

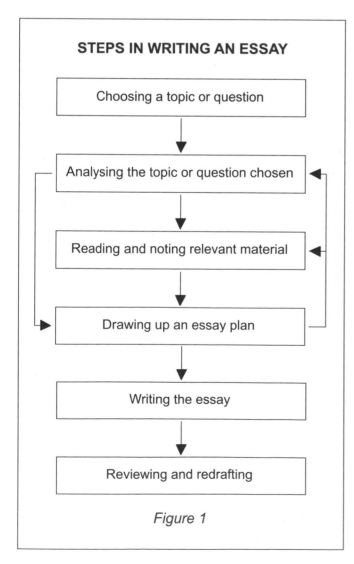

STEPS IN WRITING AN ESSAY

Choosing a topic or question

Analysing the topic or question chosen

Reading and noting relevant material

Drawing up an essay plan

Writing the essay

Reviewing and redrafting

Figure 1

Some students are alert to these subtleties of phrasing and direct their thinking accordingly. Others, however, lack this awareness: without guidance in dissecting assignment questions, they will be prone to take a question as a broad invitation to write on a theme rather than as a call to address a tightly specified topic.

Furthermore, almost any assignment question at undergraduate level will be tacit to greater or lesser degrees: what is required often goes beyond the surface meaning of the words appearing in the question.[5] Students may be invited, for example, to 'discuss', 'consider', 'review' or 'examine' a particular issue, but dictionary definitions of commonplace terms such as these will be of limited value:

> I felt pretty satisfied with my essay. I thought I'd get a brilliant mark for it. So I was really put off when I saw the lecturer's comments. I just thought it was what the essay said: "What limits a person's ability to do two things at once?" Not why, or how it was done. What I did I thought was very relevant, but the lecturer wanted 'how' and 'why' factors, and I didn't quite answer that.

At base, then, all assignment questions can be thought of as similar regardless of how they are worded. All carry with them the implicit expectation that the conventions of written academic discourse in the discipline concerned – weighing, analysing, assessing critically, evaluating systematically, as a historian or geologist or linguist would do – will be followed.

When, therefore, a student's essay seems to lack 'relevance', or simply fails to 'answer the question', the problem may well lie beyond inattention to the particular assignment question or topic set. As we shall see, the student may not yet have grasped what is expected of an undergraduate assignment in Politics or Zoology, or whatever the discipline concerned may be.

---

*Can you recall the ways in which expectations of essay-writing varied across the different subjects you studied as an undergraduate? It is a useful thinking exercise that you might try out with your students as part of a tutorial: how does an essay or other kind of coursework assignment in **this** subject differ from those in other subjects taken by your students?*

Reading and Note-Taking

Though it is sometimes possible for students to base their coursework solely on material which they have gleaned from lectures, tutorials and associated reading, most assignments call for additional reading to extend as well as consolidate students' knowledge of the topic set. Reading of this kind can however take various forms: some coursework essays, for example, involve skimming through a large number of books and articles in search of relevant material, while others demand close and meticulous attention to one or two core texts. And generally speaking, students will also need to make notes of material they are likely to make use of in their completed assignments.

Here again, differences show up in students' reading and note-taking practices. Compare the following comments, by two second-year History students:

> Sometimes I just go through a book very quickly and just jot down fact after fact, events, what people actually did and said, quotes from the time. And then I have a good body of things that I can then use to support what I want to say. So in a book I'm looking for A, his argument, and then B, facts and evidence.

> I never think that what I'm reading is relevant. I find it really hard to say 'Well, that's OK, I can put that sort of thing in', and 'That's not OK'. I just ... can't do it. I don't know why. I end up putting things down just because somebody else has written about them in a book. I just go round in circles for days and days and days.

Reviewing and Planning

For most students, the next step is to review the material which has been gathered and to draw up some kind of plan. This is not, however, universal. Some students, probably a small minority, thrive on a process of drafting and redrafting parts of the assignment in-between completing the background reading. And some, also in a minority, get by without making formal plans whether because they have already mapped out the essay in their head or, in sharp contrast, because they feel no sense of control over their essay-writing:

> I never do plans for any of my essays. They just happen. I do the usual reading and find a few quotes. I like to start off with a quote, because it's usually right. (Laughs)

But the great majority of students, perhaps because it was drummed into them at school, do regularly make some kind of plan of what they are going to write. This may take various forms:

- **a rough sketch**, cataloguing only some of the likely essay content, or not attempting to order points in sequence;

- **a basic plan**, outlining and ordering all of the key points;

- **an extended plan**, which takes the basic plan a stage further by numbering all the notes for ease of reference, and is thus particularly attractive to students who accumulate large quantities of notes;

- **an evolving plan** which, unlike its counterparts, precedes reading and notetaking, and is modified as work on the essay develops.

With the possible exception of the last of these four, however, which type of plan a student pursues does not in itself seem to matter a great deal. Much more crucial is what it is that the plan seems directed towards: in other words, the student's notion of what will make for a good essay.

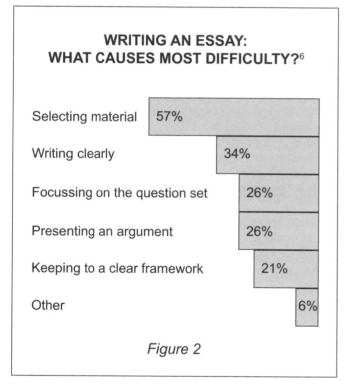

WRITING AN ESSAY: WHAT CAUSES MOST DIFFICULTY?[6]

Selecting material — 57%
Writing clearly — 34%
Focussing on the question set — 26%
Presenting an argument — 26%
Keeping to a clear framework — 21%
Other — 6%

Figure 2

Drafting and Writing Up

The decisive step, actually writing the essay or assignment, creates many competing demands – and thus sources of difficulty – for students, as *figure 2* suggests.

Differences in students' assignment-writing skills show up vividly in the extent to which they feel at ease with their introductions and, most acutely of all, their conclusions. For some, working towards a satisfying conclusion becomes second-nature:

> Conclusions are just, you've really got to just tie everything together, you've got all your strands of argument. But the conclusions, since I've come to university, have become less important, I think, 'cos your argument should be developing all the way through the essay anyway.

For others, conclusions are their slough of despond:

> Sometimes I can finish with a quote, sometimes I can sum up with my own feelings, or sometimes it just kind of gets to where there's nothing more to write, but you can't think of anything to sum up with.

> I might draw a conclusion, if I have time, and draw all the threads together. If not, I might just finish, you know, just finish, like that.

> *What makes for an effective introduction ... and an effective conclusion, in a coursework assignment in your subject? How could you best convey to your students that this is what is expected of them?*

Reviewing and Redrafting

And what of reviewing and redrafting? It seems that while there are some students who draft and redraft an essay several times, the commonest strategy is probably that of the rough draft followed by the 'clean copy', where the handwriting is neater, there are fewer crossings-out, and minor changes have been made to style and content and errors of grammar, spelling or punctuation remedied. Few students, it seems, practise the kind of thoroughgoing revision which involves reordering large segments of text, whether through lack of time or expertise or because they do not view what they have written as something which can be fashioned and refashioned to achieve their purposes.

In theory, the arrival of the word-processor should have stimulated more far-reaching revision, since it makes the task of modifying and rearranging text so much more straightforward. What little evidence we have, however, comes from a U.S. study[7] which found that undergraduates who word-processed their assignments made little use of 'cut-and-paste' keys – which suggests that their revision practices were directed towards altering words, phrases or sentences rather than more ambitious structural changes.

Conceptions of Essay-Writing

The six steps outlined here provide useful pathways from which to approach and understand assignment-writing. They help draw attention to the specific demands which an essay or similar coursework assignment poses at successive stages, and in so doing they serve to underscore its overall complexity.

Yet my own research on undergraduate essay-writing in the arts and social sciences (from which the illustrative student comments above have largely been taken) suggests that there is a more fundamental and overarching difference between students as writers of essays and other kinds of assignments. This difference is one of *conception*: how students in a given discipline conceive of what an essay is and what essay-writing entails.

In essence, essay-writing in higher education is an apprenticeship in what we might call 'academic discourse' – the conventions which govern how subject specialists communicate their ideas, theories and insights, and which determine what constitutes a plausible or at least acceptable mode of argument. In the context of essay-writing, academic discourse generally has three main characteristics:

- an overriding concern to interpret and make meaning through the presentation of arguments;

- careful attention to the marshalling of relevant and valid facts, examples and other kinds of evidence to substantiate or refute arguments and interpretations;

- a structure or organisational framework which has not been chosen arbitrarily, but is instead designed to present arguments and evidence in a coherent and logically appropriate form.

Some of the students who took part in my research had successfully grasped the nature of academic discourse. For them, essay-writing was at base an interpretive activity concerned with the disciplined pursuit of meaning. This meant that in History, for example, essay-writing was conceived of as a question of *argument,* coherently presented and well substantiated:

[In my preparatory reading] I try to find the author's own particular view, his argument, and also really just to really plunder it for facts. Whether the facts that he gives, you know, whether I agree with his argument or not, I think that the main thing in an historical essay anyway is that you make a case and back it up with actual facts of what happened, and evidence.

Being able to construct an argument, that's where for me, this plan sheet here is the key because I get everything in a logical order where everything's building up, you know, and point 1, boom, boom, boom, like that. And so I try to aim that, come the end of the essay, no matter what they thought before that, the logic of the argument and the evidence produced is such that, even if they don't agree with my interpretation, they've got to say it's reasonably argued.

But essay-writing did not have this interpretive character for many other students:

I tried to cover all the different areas. But one of the tutor's criticisms of the essay was why did I just keep going from one to the other. But I thought that's what I was supposed to do.

I'm not quite sure what [studying History at university] is about. I don't think we get a lot of our own ideas into it. I know we're supposed to, but we seem to be reading books, and criticising what people think, more than actually ... I don't know. It just seems to me as though you're reading about a period, and trying to fit your reading into an essay. It just seems like a lot of facts more than anything else.

Students such as these had not grasped the nature of academic discourse. They were aware of the various elements that played a significant role in essay-writing – advancing thoughts and ideas, drawing on factual information and findings from research or scholarship, and assembling both of these into an organised whole – but they saw these as discrete rather than as elements which could be integrated into a coherent and substantiated argument. Their concerns as essay-writers were thus targeted at what seemed to be more manageable (but less intellectually exacting) goals: an essay as the expression of a personal *viewpoint,* only loosely anchored in the available facts; or an essay as simply an *arrangement* of facts and ideas.

These differences in students' conceptions of essay-writing have a number of practical implications:

- It is difficult to see how repeated practice in writing essays will *of itself* bring about a significant improvement in the quality of written work of students who do not conceive of essay-writing as academic discourse. Indeed, repeated practice which leaves an inadequate conception unchallenged may simply reinforce it (and thus make any shift in conception progressively harder to bring about).

- The procedures students follow in writing an essay seem closely bound up with the conceptions they hold. In consequence, the planning activities of students who are seeking to advance arguments (and thus, for example, testing out possible interpretations against the available evidence) will be very different from those of students who approach the generation of ideas and the culling of reading material as though each were separate rather than interrelated tasks. Simply advising students to "make a plan" – or indeed offering any advice on technique which considers means in isolation from ends – is therefore unlikely to be effective.

- Nor, as we shall see later, will feedback from tutors *necessarily* prompt a change in conception, since such comments take for granted a mode of academic discourse which some students have yet to share.

- Students' conceptions are shaped not only by their assignment work but also by their learning experiences within tutorials and in their preparatory and follow-up reading. The latter can therefore be used by tutors as opportunities to help students gain a better understanding of academic discourse.

In the rest of this chapter, the focus shifts from student to tutor. Having reviewed what is known about students' assignment-writing, we now look at how you can build on these research findings in preparing for, marking and commenting on students' essays.

GROUNDWORK

Some aspects of assessing students' coursework can probably only be adequately learnt 'on the job', by gaining direct and first-hand experience of what is required. But there are other things which you as a tutor really need to know or to find out *before* students embark on their essays.

First, there are the basic facts about the assignment itself. In first- and second-year courses, as we have just seen, students are not at liberty to formulate their own theme but work to essay titles or topics set by course lecturers. You will therefore have to make sure that you know what the set topics or titles are and what scope students have to choose between them. You will need to know what deadline has been set for the submission of the assignment and, equally importantly, by what date you will be expected to have marked and returned the work to the students. And you will need to check what is required of students in terms of format and presentation, for example:

- What guidelines govern the format in which essays should be submitted – e.g. minimum width of margin, use of single- or double-spacing between lines, overall length to be aimed at (or perhaps not exceeded), whether the use of headings and sub-headings is encouraged or discouraged?

- To what extent will students be expected to display a familiarity with key works or 'essential reading' ... and at least some acquaintance with 'background reading' or other relevant material?

- How should references to the literature be cited in the body of the text and at the end?

- Should the essays be typed or word-processed, as many departments now require?

Second, you will need to be well-informed about the faculty or departmental policies and practices which have a particular bearing on coursework assessment. The most fundamental of these have to do with the marks to be given to students. In many universities there is a standard university-wide marking scheme (see for example *figure 3*), but these are usually designed to ensure that all students' marks across the full range of courses are recorded in a common framework. Such schemes do not normally attempt to specify what standards these various marks represent within a given department, programme of study or course unit.

AN EXAMPLE OF A UNIVERSITY-WIDE MARKING SCHEME

Final Honours		Non-Honours	
1 Honours Class	2 Mark	3 Grade	4 Description
I	75-100	A	Very Good
II.1	65-74	B	Good
II.2	55-64	C	Satisfactory
III	50-54	D	Marginal Pass
Fail	(45-49	E	Marginal Fail
	(35-44	F	Clear Fail
	(0-34	G	Bad Fail

Figure 3

Guidance on the latter can be sought in a number of ways. In some courses, the qualities looked for in students' coursework and examination answers are discussed in a course handbook or circulated to students in the form of a handout. In others, the criteria to be used in assessing a particular assignment are notified to students alongside a list of titles or topics, or are set out on a specially prepared pro forma (see *Marking and Commenting* below). Whatever the case, you should regard the course leader or your teaching supervisor as the main source of advice on the criteria and standards you will be expected to apply.

Then there is the question of established coursework procedures and practices, which will often vary from one course to another and therefore also need to be clarified. Under what circumstances can a student be granted an extension to a submission deadline, for instance, and from whom must permission be obtained? Are there penalties for late submission? What kinds of feedback, how much, and in what form, can students reasonably expect? What procedure should be followed if you are uncertain about a particular mark, or if one of your students wishes to lodge an appeal against the mark he or she has been given?

Thirdly, there is the all-important subject dimension. You cannot assess students' work fairly unless you have a good grasp of what they ought to know by a given stage in the course, and a clear sense of what they should be able to achieve in their assignments by dint of further study and reading. What will actually be necessary on your part to close this gap will depend on how familiar you already are with the subject-matter covered by the course and the course materials themselves. It is quite probable, however, that you will need to do at least some of the following:

- attend the lectures;

- study the course handbook, the class handouts and any other relevant course materials;

- make sure you are well-acquainted with whatever recommended reading forms an essential backcloth to the assignments set;

- check library holdings of recommended reading, and particularly of multiple copies of essential material, so that you have some feel for what most students will realistically be able to follow up in their preparatory reading and note-taking.

Why not now take a moment or two to review what advance groundwork you will need to do? What aspects of coursework essays are you already familiar with ... and what will you need to check out?

BRIEFING AND ADVISING STUDENTS

Like you, your students will need to be well-briefed at the outset if they are to use their time on the assignment productively. It is therefore instructive to consider *what* they will want to have clarified, *how* you can best brief them, and *when* advice from you is likely to be particularly helpful.

Clarifying What?

Your students will obviously need to have the same basic factual information at their fingertips as you, i.e. they will need to know about topics, titles, deadlines, format and presentation for the particular assignment concerned. And if they are not yet acquainted with departmental procedures and policies surrounding coursework, they will need to be told about those too.

Most importantly of all, they may need guidance on how they should set about preparing and writing their assignments. As we have already seen, students are often uncertain about what is expected of them in the coursework they submit and how they might best achieve this. But precisely what guidance your tutees will welcome and will need will depend on a variety of factors, including:

- what stage they are at in their undergraduate studies – since for example second-year students will obviously be much more familiar with what is required than students in the first term of their first year;

- whether the particular essay or other assignment for which you are responsible is of a kind they have encountered previously and have some experience of;

- what guidance they have already been given, and in what forms – a point to which we shall return shortly;

- how confident they are, as individuals, in their own writing abilities, and how satisfied they are with the marks they have typically been getting up to that point in the course.

The conclusion to be drawn at this point is simply put. Don't fall into the trap of assuming in advance that you know what your students can and can't do well – and above all, avoid thinking that it is your job to tell them everything they might need to know about writing essays or any other kind of assignment. Too much advice, especially when it is not wanted or needed, is as unwelcome as no advice at all. A wiser stratagem is to :

- establish what guidance they have already been given;

- ensure that you give them opportunities to raise the queries that are uppermost in their minds;

- be alert to cues – especially in the first pieces of written work they submit – about which aspects of assignments most students have mastered and which they have not.

AN ASSIGNMENT CHECKLIST

(tick as appropriate)

Covering Information

My title/cover page clearly shows:

☐   my name

☐   course title and number

☐   my tutor's name

☐   the question/topic I have chosen

☐   date assignment handed in

Introduction

The introduction:

☐   sets the question/topic against a wider background

☐   clarifies my understanding of the question/topic

☐   defines key or problematic terms

☐   outlines the approach I will be taking to the question/topic

Main Text

In the main body of the assignment:

☐   my key points are clearly presented

☐   the points I make are systematically backed up by facts/evidence/examples

☐   quotations and references to other works are accurately cited

☐   any diagrams, figures or tables are properly labelled

Conclusion

The conclusion:

☐   brings together the main points

☐   links back to the question/topic

☐   states clearly my conclusion(s)

Style and Presentation

Overall, the assignment:

☐   reads clearly throughout

☐   makes correct use of grammar, spelling and punctuation

☐   accurately lists the background reading I have consulted

☐   is within the word-limits specified

Figure 4

Advising How and When?

Next, there is the question of how and when you can best advise your students, in ways which will complement the guidance already available to them in their course handbook and via faculty or departmental study skills workshops and books on essay-writing (see chapter 12, *Sources and Resources*).

Before they embark on the assignment, you could spend a few minutes in a tutorial suggesting how they might tackle it and answering any questions they raise; or circulate a handout offering useful tips and hints; or ask them all to make use of a self-review checklist. *Figure 4* is an example of one simple kind of checklist which depends largely on yes/no answers. *Figure 5* is rather more general, and geared to assignments which involve a large element of information-gathering, but is intended as a prompt to reflection which requires much more than box-ticking.

While they are actually working on the assignment, you could invite them to raise any major queries they have at the beginning or the end of tutorials; or you could offer to be available to individual students at set times during your working week. Some students will welcome an opportunity to spend a few minutes talking through with you their assignment plan or a partial essay draft. For your part, however, you will need to set clear time-boundaries if you are to avoid getting swamped ... and if you are to avoid being so supportive to some students that you virtually answer the question for them, with the result that the assignment calls for very little real effort on their part.

Once the assignment has been marked and returned, there are various ways in which to back up the feedback which students will get from your written comments (see below). Whatever you decide to do, a useful rule-of-thumb is that telling students what is required is usually less effective than showing them how and explaining why. Bibliographic citation is a case in point. Students are much more likely to grasp the conventions of referencing if you explain why it is necessary to acknowledge the work of others and show them examples of good practice.

> *Do you feel you have a clear sense of what guidance on assignments your students have already been given? If you do, what additional guidance would they most welcome from you, do you think ... and how could you best provide it?*

┌───┐

**TACKLING AN ASSIGNMENT:
NINE QUESTION-STEPS FOR STUDENTS**

What do I need to do?
(formulate and analyse need)

Where could I go?
(identify and appraise likely sources)

How do I get to the information?
(trace and locate individual resources)

Which resources shall I use?
(examine, select and reject individual sources)

How shall I use the resources?
(interrogate resources)

What should I make a record of?
(record and store information)

Have I got the information I need?
(interpret, analyse, synthesise, evaluate)

How should I present it?
(present, communicate)

What have I achieved?

Figure 5

└───┘

MARKING AND COMMENTING

Of all the challenges of university teaching, marking (and commenting on) students' work is perhaps the stiffest as well as one of the most rewarding. It calls for intense and prolonged concentration, since each assignment must not only be carefully scrutinised in its own right, but also weighed and considered in the light of all the other assignments being assessed. And although the outcome in each case is a single mark, that mark is more than simply a rough-and-ready impression of the standard achieved: it represents a rounded judgment which takes account of how well the student has met each of the various criteria which have been adopted for that particular assignment.

Familiarisation with the assessment criteria to be applied is self-evidently a *sine qua non* of good marking. As far as most courses are concerned, these criteria are likely to include:

- criteria common to undergraduate assignments in a wide range of disciplines – e.g. use of

argument, organisation and presentation of material, style and 'English', i.e. grammar, spelling and punctuation;

- criteria which are discipline-specific (such as use of secondary sources in History, synthesising research findings in Psychology or Biochemistry, or appropriate use of textual illustration in literary criticism);

- criteria associated with a particular kind of assignment (e.g. mastery of the conventions of a book review, or breadth and depth of coverage in a review of the literature).

Figure 6 is one example of a set of criteria – in this instance, devised specifically for assessing English Literature essays.

For the new tutor confronting criteria such as these for the first time, it is not just a matter of acquainting oneself with the criteria as set out in their printed form, but also of finding out – usually in consultation with the course leader – how they are applied in practice. What are the relative weightings of each criterion, for example, given that however fluent the style in a particular student's essay may be, it is likely to have much less impact on the final grade than the strength and coherence of the argument presented? And what counts as 'good' or 'very good' use of recommended reading in, say, the first term of a first-year course?

Marking

Beyond being familiar with the criteria, how can you try to ensure that you mark well? The art of good marking is to approach it slowly and carefully, not rushing into hasty judgments and building in a series of checks on your accuracy and consistency. Here are a few pointers:

Getting started ...

- don't even try to mark the first few essays you read; instead, spend some time getting a broad feel for the standards the students have reached and the different ways in which they have approached the assignment;

- keep a copy of the assessment criteria for that piece of work close at hand, and refer to it frequently as a check on your consistency.

Once you have got a reasonable impression of overall standards ...

- work through each essay in turn, noting down the *provisional* mark which it merits (but do not

---

ASSESSMENT CRITERIA FOR AN ENGLISH LITERATURE ESSAY[8]

Knowledge

Text	deep, thorough, detailed knowledge	☐	☐	☐	☐	☐	superficial knowledge
Author	wide knowledge used in analysis	☐	☐	☐	☐	☐	knowledge lacking or not used
Genre	wide knowledge used in analysis	☐	☐	☐	☐	☐	knowledge lacking or not used
Historical and social context	wide knowledge used in analysis	☐	☐	☐	☐	☐	knowledge lacking or not used

Essay

Structure	clear, logical structure	☐	☐	☐	☐	☐	confused list
Quotations	correct, purposeful use, properly referenced	☐	☐	☐	☐	☐	references lacking or incorrect
Other sources	wide range, relevant, properly referenced	☐	☐	☐	☐	☐	none or irrelevant
Grammar, spelling	correct	☐	☐	☐	☐	☐	many errors

Personal

Response to text	vivid, personal	☐	☐	☐	☐	☐	no response
Viewpoint	clearly expressed	☐	☐	☐	☐	☐	viewpoint lacking or unoriginal
Creativity	imaginative, surprising	☐	☐	☐	☐	☐	predictable

Critical theory

Understanding	clear grasp	☐	☐	☐	☐	☐	no grasp
Use of methods	wide range appropriately used	☐	☐	☐	☐	☐	range limited, inappropriately used

Figure 6

write this on the essay yet – you may need to modify it up or down);

- you may find it useful at the same time to jot down the main reasons for each of your provisional marks (as something you can quickly refer back to when you are reviewing your provisional marks);

- avoid getting too bogged down with a single essay that turns out to be an especially tricky one to mark – it may be easier to come back to it later when you have a clear picture of all the other essays.

When you have worked through all the essays, you will need to review your provisional marks. The first thing to check is your reliability. This is simply done by sorting the essays into separate piles for each provisional grade, and reviewing a sample of each. Are all the A's or B's or C's actually of a similar standard, or should some of the provisional grades

be raised or lowered? Are you still convinced that any essays which failed to earn a pass mark are quite so unsatisfactory?

Secondly, it is wise to check the overall pattern of marks. Technically speaking, any set of marks can be appraised in terms of the mean (where does the average lie, and is this appropriate?) and the spread (are the marks too tightly bunched?). If you only have a small number of essays to assess – no more than a dozen, say – it is at least possible that you had been given an untypically high number of very good or very poor ones, or that almost all of them happened to deserve the same mark. But the probability is that you have not yet struck the happy balance that lies somewhere between the parsimony of Ebenezer Scrooge and the all-forgiving nature of Mother Teresa. There really is no alternative but to take a second and closer look at the essays, paying particular attention to the criteria on which your initial judgments were based.

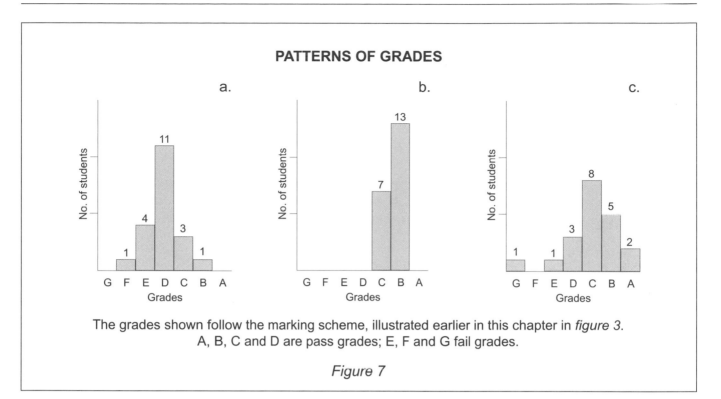

PATTERNS OF GRADES

a.   b.   c.

The grades shown follow the marking scheme, illustrated earlier in this chapter in *figure 3*. A, B, C and D are pass grades; E, F and G fail grades.

Figure 7

Yet however carefully you approach the task of marking, there may be one or two very hard nuts to crack: an essay that is a bizarre mixture of the very good and the downright bad, handwriting that even a GP would blush at, or nagging doubts about whether a student might have dabbled in plagiarism. These are not issues to be resolved by you alone. In such cases, you should seek the advice of the course leader or whichever member of staff has the formal responsibility of supervising your work as an assessor.

*Figures 7a, b and c show the patterns of grades notionally awarded to three groups, each comprising 20 students. These different grade patterns **might** have arisen by chance, of course, but which of the three is more likely to be valid?*

Commenting

Part of the feedback which students get on their written work is the mark or grade itself. This provides a necessary reference-point, signalling the overall standard which has been achieved. In higher education, however, coursework marks are always accompanied by more direct feedback in the form of written comments. These comments normally take the form of general comments on the assignment as a whole (which are usually made on a separate sheet), and specific comments in the body of the text on everything from spelling to clarity of

expression or the accuracy of a particular fact or quotation.

Strategies for making specific comments on essays are to some extent a matter of individual preference. My personal quirk is never to use red ink because of its associations with stringent criticism, but the green felt-tip which I once opted for (rather too high-mindedly, perhaps?) has now given way to a soft pencil, so that students can rub out any offending comments later if they wish. Nor am I too bothered by errors in spelling, punctuation or grammar, provided these are occasional rather than all-pervading. I tend simply to circle or underline the error in passing, though I recognise that for some of my colleagues – especially those teaching English, Linguistics, or foreign languages – this would not suffice.

But whatever your own preferences are, style and tone are of paramount importance. For no matter how accurate or valid a tutor's comment may be, if it is couched in dismissive or bitingly critical terms it will leave the student feeling hurt or angry rather than receptive. Phrasing specific comments in the form of questions (as, for example, in *figure 8*) is one way of encouraging students to respond positively to feedback.

General comments

General comments tend to be of two interrelated kinds. How well did the student tackle this particular assignment – the topic or question set, the subject-matter concerned, and the form in which

COMMENTS ON AN ASSIGNMENT

Would it help to draw a (Why) does this occur?
sharper distinction between
this second question of   Posner has made a distinction between automatic and attentive
'why' and the earlier   (parallel or serial) processing. He hypothesises that the
question of 'under what   consequences of this attentive state is that it consumes a portion
circumstances'?   of the "limited resource capacity" of the system, which, in effect,
                            places constraints on the amount of processing that can be carried
                            out at that given moment by another modality. He postulates further
                            that this induces "inertia" into the processing mechanism. The
                            attentive state of the dominant modality is self-perpetuating as it
You're right to see this   takes time and effort to switch from one modality to another.
point as a crucial one -   Turvey (1978) has summarised it thus:_ "With respect to the inertia
but how would YOU   induced by the mode of attentive (serial) processing, Posner et al.
have summarised it?   (1976) have recently interpreted the peculiar phenomenon of visual
                            capture as being indicative of an asymmetry between switching from
                            vision to another modality, and switching from another modality to
                            vision. When the information for vision and another modality are in
                            conflict, vision is the likely victor" (Turvey 78 p. 206).

                            As previously mentioned, if a person is not 'set' to vision, he is
                            at a disadvantage when it comes to switching in terms of time.
Why 'hopefully'?   (Hopefully) it could be hypothesised that, for survival reasons during
                            the evolutionary process, human attention has become set to vision
                            (e.g. it was more advantageous for homo erectus to run when he saw a
                            sabre-toothed tiger, rather than wait about to hear him roar or feel
                            his fur a few feet away). Turvey has called this bias 'soft-ware'
                            as opposed to 'hard-ware', this is explained by saying that if
                            prismatically distorted vision accompanies haptic exploration (and
                            vision is set to attend) then the haptic system undergoes adaption;
                            but if it is the haptic system which is attended to then vision is
                            'recalibrated' (Kelso, Cook, Olsen and Epstein, 1976). In the
                            absence of purposeful 'set' of any one modality, vision is attended
                            to by choice.

A punchline like this   { To all intent and purposes, research seems to indicate what Hugh
may be hard to resist.   { Heffner knew all along - 'man is a visual animal'.
But how confident are you that you've said enough by way of conclusion?
Do you really feel you've done justice to all your earlier observations on the research literature?

Figure 8

it was expected to be submitted? And how well did the student meet the requirements of academic discourse in this discipline at this level – e.g. by setting out a distinctive interpretation or argument, plausibly supported and coherently presented?

General comments on an assignment are most likely to be helpful to a student when:

- a balance is struck between criticism of shortcomings and praise for what has been done well – not as easy as it sounds, since most

of us have an inbuilt tendency to find fault rather than to applaud; as a corrective, you might try writing your general comments under two headings: "Good points" and "Could be improved"[9];

- broad-brush observations – e.g. about the structure of the essay or the student's use of quotations or references – are explicitly linked to specific comments in the body of the assignment, thus illustrating for the student precisely what you mean;

- you refer a student to other resource materials (a guide to essay-writing in the subject concerned) where her or his work has serious shortcomings such as a lack of grasp of argument, the use of evidence or confusion about the functions of introductions or conclusions.

In some undergraduate courses, it should be noted, general comments are being replaced by or complemented with assignment 'attachments' or pro formas of the kind illustrated in *figure 9*. These can provide a straightforward and economical way of giving feedback in a form which directly relates a tutor's observations to the criteria being used to evaluate the assignment. And since tutors normally retain a copy of each completed pro forma or attachment for their own records, it is a simple matter to survey these in order to gain a precise picture of the collective strengths and weaknesses of one's tutees – and thus to establish what additional guidance is likely to have the greatest impact.

ASSIGNMENT ATTACHMENTS: AN EXAMPLE[10]

Energy and Life Systems

Student's name: Assignment grade:

Itemised Rating Scale
(ticked when applicable)

STRUCTURE

Essay relevant to topic	☐	☐	☐	☐	Essay has little relevance
Topic covered in depth	☐	☐	☐	☐	Superficial treatment of topic

ARGUMENT

Accurate presentation of evidence	☐	☐	☐	☐	Much evidence inaccurate or questionable
Logically developed argument	☐	☐	☐	☐	Essay rambles and lacks continuity
Original and creative thought	☐	☐	☐	☐	Little evidence of originality

STYLE

Fluent piece of writing	☐	☐	☐	☐	Clumsily written
Succinct writing	☐	☐	☐	☐	Unnecessarily repetitive

PRESENTATION

Legible and well set out work	☐	☐	☐	☐	Untidy and difficult to read
Reasonable length	☐	☐	☐	☐	Over/under length

SOURCES

Adequate acknowledgement of sources	☐	☐	☐	☐	Inadequate acknowledgement of sources
Correct citation of references	☐	☐	☐	☐	Incorrect referencing

MECHANICS

Grammatical sentences	☐	☐	☐	☐	Several ungrammatical sentences
Correct spelling throughout	☐	☐	☐	☐	Much incorrect spelling
Effective use of figures and tables	☐	☐	☐	☐	Figures and tables add little to argument
Correct use of units and quantitites	☐	☐	☐	☐	Some units incorrect

---

Explanation and Comments

Tutor:

Figure 9

Follow-Up

Comments on assignments are not the only means of providing students with feedback. Indeed there are advantages in combining written or pro forma comments with some form of follow-up guidance, since many students – and particularly those with a heavy load of coursework – may be prone to see each assignment as an isolated task "with no past or future".[11]

There are various possibilities open to you. You could spend part of a tutorial giving a short 'post-mortem' on issues of wide relevance emerging from the marked assignments; or achieve the same end in the form of a handout; or encourage those who are keen to have further guidance to make an appointment with you. If you opt for a post-mortem, however, remind yourself firmly that you are not actually dissecting a corpse. You will kill off your students' enthusiasm if you castigate individuals in public or dwell on everyone's shortcomings. It is much better to focus on what was done well (and why), or to draw attention to the different but equally effective ways in which problems raised by the assignment had been tackled.

Finally, there is the question of record-keeping. It is of course essential to keep an accurate record of marks or grades, which will have to be passed on to the course leader or the departmental office. It is also a good idea (especially if a pro forma is not being used) to keep some record of your general comments. You may want to refer back to these at a later date, to check, for example, whether a particular student's work has been regularly dogged by the same shortcomings – and thus whether special action may be needed to bring about real improvement.

No less importantly, reviewing these records at a later date may help to bring home to you what your tutees were able to do in their written work by the end of the course that they could not accomplish when it began. This is a valuable reminder of the point made at the beginning of this chapter: assessment is about learning as well as grading.

REFERENCES

1. Except where otherwise indicated, all of the research findings and quotations from interviews with students cited in this chapter originate in the following: Hounsell, D. (1984). Learning and essay-writing. In: Marton, F., Hounsell, D. and Entwistle, N., eds. *The Experience of Learning.* Edinburgh: Scottish Academic Press pp. 103-123; Hounsell, D. (1987). Essay-writing and the quality of feedback. In: Richardson, J.T.E. et al., eds. *Student Learning: Research in Education and Cognitive Psychology.* Milton Keynes: SRHE & Open University Press pp. 109-119; Hounsell, D. (1988). Towards an anatomy of academic discourse: meaning and context in the undergraduate essay. In: Saljo, R., ed. *The Written World: Studies in Literate Thought and Action.* Berlin: Springer Verlag pp. 161-177.; Hounsell, D. and Murray, R. (1992). *Essay Writing for Active Learning.* Sheffield: CVCP Universities' Staff Development Unit.

2. Thorndike, E.L. (1911). *Animal Intelligence.* New York: Hafner. Cited in: McKeachie, W.J. (1974). The decline and fall of the laws of learning. *Educational Researcher* 3.3, pp. 7-11.

3. Rhys, J. (1968). *Wide Sargasso Sea.* London: Penguin. p. 81.

4. Norton, L.S. (1990). Essay-writing: what really counts? *Higher Education* 20.4 (1990) pp. 411-442.

5. See Polanyi, M. (1967). *The Tacit Dimension* London: Routledge and Kegan Paul

6. Norton, L.S., op. cit.

7. Daiute, C. (1986). Physical and cognitive factors in revising: insights from studies with computers. *Research into the Teaching of English* 20, pp. 141-159.

8. From Gibbs, G. and Jenkins, A., eds. (1992). *Teaching Large Classes in Higher Education: How to Maintain Quality with Reduced Resources* London: Kogan Page, p.47.

9. Beard, R. (1972). *Teaching and Learning in Higher Education.* 2nd edn. Harmondsworth: Penguin.

10. This assignment pro forma was devised at Murdoch University in Western Australia.

11. Roe, E. (1974). *Assignments.* Brisbane: University of Queensland, Tertiary Education Institute p. 60.

Chapter 7
Supporting and Advising Students
Kate Day

INTRODUCTION

For most demonstrators 'supporting and advising students' constitutes the main substance of their work – what they informally and continuously do as practical classes proceed. For tutors, on the other hand, who are characteristically concerned with teaching groups of students, the provision of support and advice is more of a supplementary – and not necessarily anticipated – activity. Accordingly, this chapter is mainly intended for tutors, although demonstrators will doubtless find aspects of direct interest to them too.

There are several reasons why as a part-time teacher you are likely to get involved in supporting and advising students – whether during class time or on a more individual basis.

- Tutorial teaching is intended to be interactive and entails helping students explore their understanding and consolidate their mastery, not just of the course content, but also of the skills required to carry out the tasks appropriate to particular academic disciplines.

- First year undergraduates are finding their feet in an unfamiliar environment. They may take some time to appreciate university and departmental procedures, or what is expected of them as learners and how they should go about studying.

- Tutorials and practical classes provide points of regular contact between teaching staff and students, and students often perceive tutors or demonstrators as particularly approachable and able to be of assistance.

The contexts within which teachers in different departments work vary in a number of respects – for example, in how well documented the course is, whether tutorials and practicals are expected to follow a set pattern, and the students' attitudes and competencies. These departmental differences, combined with variations in teaching styles and preferences, will clearly affect the approach any one part-time teacher takes to supporting and advising students.

What is certain is that tutors and demonstrators are much better placed to provide guidance than they sometimes appreciate. They have a grasp of the key concepts and basic skills in their discipline, and will have accumulated, though not necessarily consciously, a store of useful information both about the subject and about studying. It is true that their own experiences as academically successful students may be rather different from some of the people they are now teaching and which may make them hesitant to offer advice. Nor will they want to be prescriptive about specific approaches to learning and study methods, since individuals need to develop systems suited to their own aspirations and ways of working. But tutors and demonstrators usually do have a better idea than many undergraduates how to avoid getting into difficulties, to cope with those that arise, to seek further information or to access additional resources.

More problematic for part-time teachers, whose priority commitments lie elsewhere, is setting fair and sensible limits on what assistance is given and how much time it takes up. Establishing and maintaining an appropriate balance is particularly hard for those who are new to the job or who especially enjoy helping students. While the demands of students for attention tend to fluctuate over the course of the academic year, according to the pressures exerted by coursework, tests and exams for example, other kinds of difficulties can be around at any time.[1] Moreover, teachers sometimes have to be pro-active and explicitly encourage students to consult with them, because of the general reluctance of students to impose. But if students' needs are potentially open-ended, tutors' and demonstrators' responsibilities are not, and do not extend to trying to meet every eventuality. There are many other staff and services within the university, as well as fellow students, who can often be more appropriate sources of advice and support.

The rest of this chapter provides some ideas about:

- what can be done, within the tutorial setting in particular, to make things clearer for students and thereby assist their progress as learners (see chapter 5 for the demonstrator's role in the practical setting);

- how tutors and demonstrators can work with students and give guidance in one-to-one consultations.

MAKING THINGS CLEARER

Once at university, undergraduates take on a new responsibility for managing their own studying. Whilst there are lectures and tutorials, assigned work and library resources to help them, whether they grasp the opportunities and realise their potential depends on their motivation, previous experience and how readily they develop strategies for coping with the requirements of a different environment. To succeed, students also need to be cued into the demands and expectations of particular subjects. This more specific orientation might concern, for example, the conventions for organising and presenting work and can be done partly through course documentation, but not entirely. Accordingly tutors are likely to lighten their consultation load if they create opportunities in tutorials (whether directly or whilst focusing on other areas of work) for encouraging students' appreciation of what they should be trying to achieve and the means whereby progress can be made. What follows are some suggestions about the general and the more specific aspects of supporting students in gearing themselves up for effective learning.

The Demands of Academic Study

The *general* aspect involves students firstly, in recognising that academic work is meant to be intellectually challenging and, secondly, having access to an appropriate repertoire of study strategies and skills.

Stressing the need for real effort and commitment, coupled with indicating ways in which over time academic tasks can be mastered, has several

beneficial effects. If uncertainty about how best to proceed is accepted by students as normal rather than exceptional, they will be more inclined to target and tackle study problems rather than attribute them to their own lack of ability. They may also adopt more realistic time scales for improving their knowledge and skills, rather than seeking magic-bullet solutions. It is the case that while the demands of managing a new personal and social life may on occasions interfere with students' academic progress, most quickly recover their equilibrium.

Guidance materials. Study skills guides abound: most book shops keep a selection in stock, and they are to be found in many libraries too. Chapter 12, *Sources and Resources,* lists some recommended titles which may well be available in your own institution. By dipping into these publications students can be helped to develop productive ways of going about their academic work. But if students are struggling with their studies, they can easily become overwhelmed by reading study skills manuals cover-to-cover or misled by thinking there are sets of fail-safe rules to follow. Clearly if tutors are able to look through some of these guides themselves, it will both stimulate their own thoughts about effective studying and make it easier to point students in suitable directions.

Workshops. Another possibility is for students to attend any study skills workshops that may be offered within the university – on such topics as effective reading, making the most of tutorials, note-taking, writing essays or preparing for exams.

Tips and hints. Although general purpose study skills guides and workshops are valuable resources, they are not geared to delivering finely grained guidance, and research studies confirm the limited value of study skills advice isolated from specific subject or course settings. It is therefore worth tutors considering what kinds of guidance would be most helpful to their students. A useful starting-point is the list of handy hints given in *figure 1*, provided care is taken by tutors to adapt the list to their students' particular needs.

*To what extent would the handy hints given in figure 1 be appropriate advice for **your** students? Which of these hints would you want to modify, or perhaps leave out altogether? And what new hints would it be important to add?*

EFFECTIVE STUDYING – HANDY HINTS?

- Split large and challenging academic tasks into more manageable chunks.
- Plan backwards from deadlines, so that you know when as well as what you need to get done.
- Be realistic about how much you can achieve and build in some flexibility.
- Schedule in recreation time, take breaks and know when it is okay not to be working.
- Think about when and where you work best, and allocate prime tasks to prime time.
- Give yourself rewards for tasks completed rather than for time spent.
- Keep an appropriate balance between work, other commitments and play.
- Develop a sense of what proportion of time and effort to give to various parts of a task.
- Engage in active debate with the materials you are studying.
- Be systematic in the organisation of lecture and other notes, and consolidate materials.
- Allow sufficient time to critically review and edit work produced for assessment.
- Become proficient in information, library, computer, numeric, linguistic or any other skills which are going to be useful to you.

Figure 1

The tutorial group. Finally, bear in mind that the tutorial itself is also an excellent setting for exploring study strategies and skills. Students can increase their appreciation of how they can support and learn from one another by, for example, sharing their varied approaches to similar academic tasks, working together on joint presentations, or giving feedback. Tutors, too, can comment within the group on common strengths and weaknesses in students' oral and written work.

Procedures and Requirements

Alongside the general demands of academic study are the more specific procedures, expectations, and requirements associated with a particular course. In thinking about what guidance students might need, a first step is for tutors to become well-acquainted with the course themselves. You might do this by, for example:

- getting hold of and reading the course documentation – course booklet, handouts,

essay lists, and so on, so that you know what is available in written form to students (who won't always be as thorough);

- finding out from the course leader and other tutors about departmental practices and conventions, any changes made to course content or process, how tutorials fit with the rest of the course, and what guidance is given for their conduct;

- taking a good look at and arranging for access to any set or recommended books for the course, checking out library holdings of books, periodicals and past exam papers;

- clarifying with course staff anything you are unsure about or mystified by, regarding either your own responsibilities or what students are supposed to do;

- making sure you know who can be relied on to provide additional information as required – tutors need their own support networks securely in place too!

You can then consider what needs to be communicated to students at appropriate points in the tutorial sequence, which might involve either reminding them of written information or providing it anew. Below are some of the possibilities, which you could adapt and add to with suggestions of your own:

- requirements governing tutorial attendance, how and when to notify a tutor of unavoidable absence, and guidelines for tutors contacting personal tutors;

- expectations of the amount of time and effort students should put into preparing for tutorials and how they can get the most out of participating;

- course expectations for the presentation and submission of written work, and extension policies and procedures;

- the circumstances in which students should make contact with a tutor and how to do this – e.g. buttonholing the tutor before or after a tutorial, leaving a note in the tutor's pigeonhole, calling by at a set time, phoning or using e-mail.

ADVISING STUDENTS ONE-TO-ONE

Despite the efforts made in classes to prevent difficulties arising, students will still sometimes present themselves or otherwise come to a teacher's attention, and need to be dealt with individually.

It may be simply a matter of giving students the right information, getting them to think through the repercussions of their own actions, offering reassurance or guiding them in an appropriate direction. But some students may have difficulty in pinpointing what is bothering them or going wrong, since they often lack a framework or vocabulary for thinking about and discussing their studying. They may need diagnostic help: to identify or disentangle problems, to put these in perspective, and to decide what is most important to try and sort out first. They may also need help in searching out their positive assets – those strengths, achievements and existing skills on which they can build.

Diagnostic help initially involves listening attentively and acting very much as a sounding board. The aim is to appreciate more readily the student's own concerns and to avoid giving a stock response. If a student finds it hard to articulate a problem, he or she will need encouragement to say more about how they go about studying or whatever is the issue. Starting with questions which focus on *who*, *what*, *when*, *where* and *how* tends to be a more productive way of discovering what is happening, rather than the kind of *why* questions that can make someone feel put on the spot. By encouraging students to separate out the facts from surrounding perceptions and feelings, they can be helped to reassess the nature of their difficulties and, hopefully, cut them down to size.

In circumstances where improving matters is less straightforward and not amenable to speedy resolution, the tutor or demonstrator should aim:

- to instil confidence without promising an elusive quick-fix;

- to offer support, but not open-ended assistance;

- to clarify with the student their respective roles in tackling the problem(s).

The student has to shoulder the major responsibility for change, but can be greatly helped to appreciate where the difficulties lie, how best to move forwards, what resources can be drawn upon, and when reasonable progress has been made. Students who have put a determined effort into improving their academic work sometimes find it hard to gauge when enough is enough, and will need to be cautioned about making demands upon themselves which are unrealistically high.

In some cases, however, it will become evident that a matter lies outside the responsibility or the competence of a teacher to deal with, and considering whether to refer a student to someone else is as much in the student's as the teacher's interest.[2] Students may need to be referred to other academic staff (e.g. the course leader, other lecturers or the personal tutor) or to support services (e.g. counselling and advice services run by the university or student bodies).

CONFIDENTIALITY

Alongside setting limits on the extent of their involvement, part-time teachers – like their full-time counterparts – need to be aware of the thorny issue of confidentiality. As a general rule students' privacy must be respected, and considerable care taken to keep confidences. When it is felt that others ought to be consulted or alerted to a student's difficulties, the teacher should inform the student and get his or her agreement before proceeding further. Another aspect of protecting students' interests and maintaining a professional stance is to avoid getting too friendly with students or gossiping and grousing, which can be divisive and unsettling for all concerned. It is unwise for tutors or demonstrators to get drawn into discussions about individual members of staff or to be other than as supportive as they can about the course and their department.

However, when an issue does arise that needs bringing to someone else's attention, such as a difficulty with the course or the department which the students generally are experiencing, there need be no inhibitons about broaching it, tactfully but assertively. For tutors and demonstrators are a vital two-way bridge between the undergraduate students and the academic staff involved in a course.

REFERENCES

1. For a good indication of the main areas within which students may benefit from assistance, see Race, P. and Brown, S. (1993) *500 Tips for Tutors*. London: Kogan Page. The section headings are General Study Skills, Starting Off and Working Together, Lectures and Written Work, Learning Resources, Various Kinds of Assessment, Life Skills.

2. For a helpful discussion of role boundaries and when to decide to refer students, see Earwaker, J. (1992). *Helping and Supporting Students*. Milton Keynes: Society for Research in Higher Education & Open University Press, pp. 78-85.

Chapter 8
Student Learning
Charles Anderson

INTRODUCTION

The other chapters in this handbook look in detail at various aspects of the work of a tutor or demonstrator and the skills of teaching. This chapter has a rather different focus. It steps back from the role of the teacher to look at how new undergraduates may view and respond to tutorials, practicals and other aspects of academic life.

As researchers and teachers we have undergone a lengthy initiation into the ways of the academic tribe, and we have a very detailed knowledge of the ground rules which govern debate and enquiry within our individual disciplines. The skills and procedures that we use as a matter of routine in our academic work and the standards that we employ to judge the quality of research in our discipline seem a natural, unproblematic, part of our life. It is difficult, therefore, for us to recapture just how new and strange an environment university seems to many entrant undergraduates, or the feelings of challenge, even threat, that they may experience. One simple, but far from trivial, theme which runs through this chapter is that matters which may appear transparent to us as academics can be quite opaque to many undergraduates. There is a need to give a very explicit account of the skills that are required to be a successful student in a particular subject and the criteria that are used to judge success or failure. It will be argued that tutors and demonstrators have a particularly crucial role to play in making explicit the demands of academic life and in delineating the skills that students are expected to acquire.

The importance of communicating expectations to new students in a clear, detailed fashion is highlighted when one considers the diversity that exists in their prior experience. Some students will have gained a fairly accurate general picture of the nature of university life from school and family, while others will have only a very vague impression of what is expected of them. It is necessary to give all beginning students a very clear account of how they are expected to study, debate and write, if the effects of these initial inequalities in preparation for university life are to be reduced.

In addition to diversity in past educational experience, there are important differences between students in their abilities, their level of confidence in their own abilities, their approaches to studying, their purposes in studying and their conceptions of learning. This chapter will explore the nature and the effects of differences between students in their purposes in, and perceptions of, studying. A number of key ideas, from the large body of research that has been done into student learning in higher education, will be presented to illuminate the way in which different students view and approach studying. These ideas will, it is hoped, provide a useful framework for developing an appropriate teaching approach with first year students in particular, and for guiding the direction that is taken in giving advice to individual students on study-related matters.

THE STUDENT'S PERSPECTIVE

Conceptions of Learning

The way in which students adapt to the demands of university life is powerfully mediated by their own conceptions, beliefs and purposes. A very important influence on the way that a student goes about studying is the conception she or he has of the nature and purposes of learning. Interview studies in which adults are asked what learning means to them have found qualitatively different conceptions.[1,2] Learning was viewed as:

1   a quantitative increase in knowledge;

2   memorizing;

3   the acquisition of facts, methods, etc. which can be retained and used when necessary;

4   the abstraction of meaning;

5   an interpretative process aimed at understanding reality.[3]

In the first three conceptions in this hierarchy the accent is on the straightforward acquisition of discrete pieces of knowledge and on simply *reproducing* information. It is not recognised that the material which is to be learnt may need to be interpreted and transformed. Learning does not involve any challenging change.

The last two conceptions imply the existence of a much more *active* learner – one who is engaging deeply with a text or a problem, incorporating new information with previous knowledge and achieving a satisfying personal sense of understanding.

Approaches to Studying

A related set of differences has been found in the *intentions* which students pursue when they are engaged on an academic task. The purpose that a student has in mind, say in reading an academic article, will affect the way that she or he goes about the task and the quality of understanding that is achieved. The term *deep approach* has been used to describe the type of learning that is associated with an intention to understand material for oneself and to interact in a critical, engaged way with content.[4,5] When students start out with this intention, they are concerned to relate new ideas to existing knowledge, to examine carefully the logic of arguments and to find organising principles to integrate their thoughts.

A very different intention guides a student who is taking a *surface approach* to a particular academic task. The intention in this case is simply to reproduce parts of the material that they are studying, and there is a much more passive acceptance of facts and ideas. Students who are adopting a *surface approach* to a task focus on memorising facts and procedures in a straightforward manner, and do not actively seek out guiding principles or structure in the material that they encounter. They fail to reflect on their purposes or learning strategies.[6]

Making Expectations Explicit

The research findings which have been reviewed in the past few paragraphs bring into focus the fact

that teachers and students may not share a common goal. Some students may need to be given the opportunity to stand back from their everyday efforts, and be encouraged to reflect on their own conceptions of learning.

It can be made clear to students, through discussion and comments on written work, that a surface, reproductive approach to a topic is not viewed as sufficient within higher education. On a more positive note, students may be alerted to the expectation that they should engage in an active dialogue with a teacher or author and use this process of interaction to develop a new understanding of particular topics. A shared understanding also needs to be established of the purposes of tutorials and practicals and the expectations and conventions that govern student participation. These are dealt with in chapters 3, 4 and 5.

Learning the Discipline

In addition to gaining a general sense of the purposes that individuals are expected to pursue in studying at university, students also need an explicit account of the criteria that are used to judge understanding within a particular discipline. This theme is highlighted and pursued in detail in chapter 6, *Marking and Commenting on Essays*.

Tutors and demonstrators also have a very important role to play in enabling students to develop a *detailed* sense of how to go about learning in a particular discipline. Books or leaflets on study skills can be of great benefit to students, but they have certain inherent limitations. Their advice necessarily has to be very general in its form, and they very often do not specify exactly how their sensible, general guidelines can be put into practice. A study skills booklet which I read recently advised students to take only "relevant" notes. No one is likely to quarrel with this common-sense piece of advice; but for a novice in a subject it may be very difficult to put this principle into practice. Sorting out what is, or is not, relevant from a mass of new information can be a very problematic business.

Teachers can demonstrate in a fine-grained way, using very specific tasks, how an entrant undergraduate can direct his or her efforts in a relevant fashion. They can indicate clearly *which* topics should be given priority and *how* one is expected to engage with these topics. Students will gain much information on what is appropriate practice in a discipline in a somewhat indirect fashion by, for example, observing the choice of topics for a tutorial, how the tutor chooses to address these topics and the way in which debate proceeds within a tutorial. On occasions, though, it may be necessary to model in a very explicit fashion how to set about the task of essay-writing, read a complex graph, score, picture or sculpture or make sense of a set of figures contained within a table.

Developing Subject Knowledge

Aside from helping to hand on the skills required for successful practice in a discipline, tutors and demonstrators can diagnose misconceptions of key concepts and move students towards a richer, more complex, understanding of subject-matter. There are opportunities within tutorials and practicals both to gain a reasonably clear sense of how students are viewing a topic and to articulate a more authoritative conception of that topic. This does not, however, imply a straightforward, one-way transmission of a more 'correct' view of a piece of knowledge to a group of students. In contrast, successful teaching and learning, like everyday conversation, requires constant adaptation to the other person's position. Students have the responsibility to wrestle to make sense of new material, including the points that a teacher is attempting to communicate. Teachers for their part have the responsibility of continually monitoring and carefully tailoring contributions to ensure that the ideas they are presenting are accessible to a student, or group of students.

Skilful teachers will on occasion take a term from a student, or a short statement in everyday language, provisionally accept this term and then proceed, sometimes in quite a gradual manner, to reformulate the student's statement in a more technically correct or discipline-appropriate manner. It will often also be useful to act in the opposite direction, and ask searching questions about key terms and concepts, to ensure that students have a very precise sense of their meaning and application. By a careful and non-threatening process of questioning, a teacher can get students to communicate their understanding of central concepts in the lecture blocks that they are studying at a particular time. It is then possible to repair or to refine their understanding of these terms.[7]

Successful teaching, then, is likely to involve an interplay between *taking out* an expert's view of a subject to students in terms that novices are likely to understand and *drawing in* students' more common-sense understandings towards expert positions within the discipline.

Problems in Understanding

One of the many functions tutorials can perform is that of allowing students to raise problems that they are having with some aspect of the content of their course. To allow exploration of problems in understanding to take place the tutor needs to schedule some time for this activity and to foster a group atmosphere in which students feel free to say that they do not understand something.

It can be difficult for someone who is new to a subject to articulate the nature of the difficulty that he or she is facing. An academically able second year student whom I interviewed, commented on the problems that students may have in the early stages of their undergraduate career in raising difficulties:

> It's all very well saying to people "ask whatever questions you want" but very often when you come to university, you don't know what questions you want to ask. So there'll be embarrassed silence and somebody'd ask when the next exams were. But that wasn't the information that we really needed to know.

As I went on to discuss this statement with her, it became clear that she was articulating a distinction between knowing that you are facing a difficulty and having a more clearly formulated problem that someone else has helped you to construct.[8] It may be necessary to assist in shaping the problem that a student is experiencing. Although it is reasonable to expect students who are well advanced in their knowledge of a subject to take on full responsibility for communicating their problems, tutors may need to take a more pro-active approach with students who are novices in a subject.

STYLES OF LEARNING AND TEACHING

Turning to another area of research that is very relevant to everyday practice, it has been found that there are distinct differences between individuals in their style of working through an academic task. Two students (or teachers for that matter) may work on the same topic and achieve a comparable level of understanding, but reach this outcome by taking quite different routes through the material. A distinction has been drawn between *serialist* and *holist* learning styles.[9] The serialist prefers a fairly narrow focus on the material that is to be mastered, building up understanding in a step-by-step logical manner. In contrast, the holist sets out to learn new material by attempting to gain a broad overview of the topic and delights in illustrations and analogies.

Another style of learning in which individuals use both global and analytical processes where appropriate is termed *versatile*. This versatile style, it is suggested, is best suited for achieving a high quality of understanding.

Problems can arise if there is a marked mismatch between the learning style of a student and that of a tutor or demonstrator. It has been noted that if teachers in higher education adopt extreme styles, either holist, or serialist, "it seems inevitable that students with the opposite style will find those classes uncongenial and difficult. Yet lecturers are free to indulge their own stylistic preferences, however extreme, while students have to make the best of relative degrees of mismatch with their own preferences".[10] To meet the marked contrast in student preferences concerning the structuring of learning, some variety in teaching is necessary. It also seems to be important to provide analogies and illustrations for the holist *and* sufficient structure and detail for the serialist.[11] Variety of experience over the course of their undergraduate career may also encourage students to adopt the *versatile* style of learning – the one which is best suited to meet the demands of studying at university.

In my own research on student views of tutorials, I have found marked differences between students in the way that they wanted tutorials to be structured. Some preferred tutorial talk which is clearly and fairly tightly focused on a topic while others preferred a more wide-ranging discussion.[12] These differences in the favoured structure for a tutorial can be seen to have parallels with the contrast which has been drawn between *holist* and *serialist* styles. To give a sense of how students commented on this matter, here are abridged quotes from two women students who were members of the same tutorial group.

> Student 1: I want it to be always very focused. — They are a waste of time if you just sit there and everyone just talks about what they feel like talking about.

> Student 2: I don't like that when tutors focus all the time because I think that's wrong — it is to me very important to understand the relationship between two things which maybe initially you don't think of relating but as you go to discussion you think oh maybe they are, and I think that's very important.

Obviously it is not feasible to have any direct matching of the learning/teaching style of a tutor and of the students in his or her group. However, tutors do need to be alert to the effects that adopting an extreme style of structuring discussion may have on some of the students in their group.

SELF-CONFIDENCE

The account that has been given so far of student learning has been a somewhat theoretical one. This concluding section of the chapter attempts to remedy that imbalance between thought and emotion and to turn attention to the, often powerful, feelings that are aroused by the need to deal with the uncertainties of a new environment. Whether individuals react fearfully, or with enthusiasm, to the challenges of a new environment is determined in large measure by the beliefs that they hold about their own ability to act effectively. People who have strong beliefs in their *self-efficacy* put more effort into new tasks and are more persistent in the face of difficulties. A firm sense of personal efficacy gives staying power.[13] This greater investment of effort does improve performance.

Conversely a lack of confidence and a fear-driven motivational style, in addition to making it harder to persist in a task, may lead to a lower quality of learning. It has been found that students who have a high *fear of failure* are more likely to adopt a *surface*, reproductive approach to learning.[14] Students are not likely to be drawn towards a view of understanding which stresses the active negotiation of new meanings if they have little confidence in their own abilities and worth as thinkers. If you lack the belief that you have something of value to contribute to others, you have little choice but to see yourself as a passive recipient of information and wisdom. A similar set of considerations applies to participation in tutorials. For the sense of self as a worthwhile participant in intellectual debates and sharing of ideas to emerge and be sustained, a learner needs to be given a 'voice' in the setting where he or she is learning and rewards for using that voice. Chapter 3, *Tutoring in Arts and Social Sciences* looks at ways in which less confident students can be encouraged to participate in tutorials and, it is hoped, thereby gain a stronger sense of their own ability to engage in debate.

Attributing Success and Failure

When we succeed, or fail, at a task there is a choice of ways in which we can explain the outcome. We can attribute success to more stable factors such as ability or to less stable factors such as effort and luck. Success can be explained in terms of *internal* factors such as ability, or effort, or to *external* features such as good teaching, or having an easy task.

Research studies have demonstrated clearly that attributing failure or difficulties to stable internal factors like ability can have a powerfully discouraging, demotivating, effect on learning. To give a concrete illustration of this general finding, a student who believes firmly that he or she does not have the ability to use computers may be very reluctant even to approach a keyboard. When students see themselves as lacking in the ability to use computers, it may therefore be important to help them to *reattribute* the source of their problems with computers or lack of willingness to use information technology. This reattribution might be to more easily changed internal features such as a *lack of effort*, or a *lack of relevant experience* or to external features such as a *lack of appropriate teaching/support*.

In the early stages of working with individual students who are experiencing difficulties in their studies, it is often very important to get a clear sense of how they themselves are accounting for the source of their problems. Where appropriate these students can then be given an alternative perspective on the origins of their difficulties and assisted to develop their skills in the ways suggested in chapter 7, *Supporting and Advising Students*.

Theories of Intelligence and Learning Goals

Pursuing the subject of perceptions of ability in somewhat greater detail, it has been shown that even in childhood individuals develop contrasting theories of intelligence[15]. Some individuals see intelligence as a *fixed trait*, and believe that they have a pre-determined level of mental abilities which cannot be readily modified, whereas other individuals view intelligence as a *malleable entity*.

Individuals who see intelligence as a fixed trait are very concerned with issues concerning ability. Their learning goals focus on gaining positive judgements and avoiding negative judgements of their intellectual competence. This close focus on their own abilities means that "confidence in their own ability must be high and must remain high if they are to choose appropriately challenging tasks and pursue them in effective ways". In contrast, individuals who believe that their abilities can be expanded and built up, have the goal of increasing their competence and focus on effort "as the means to accomplishment" and "the factor that engenders pride and satisfaction with performance".[16]

There are likely to be very distinct limits on the extent to which beliefs about ability, and associated goals, that have developed over a lifetime of schooling can be readily modified. However, the picture that teachers present of learning in a particular discipline is important here. If teachers stress that becoming competent in a discipline is a matter of gradually building up and refining a repertoire of skills, rather than the operation of some mysterious god-given talent, students are more likely to persist in their attempts to master new intellectual challenges. Similar considerations apply in developing individual students' competence in taking part in practicals or tutorials. Disabling beliefs such as "I can't think on my feet" or "I'm all fingers and thumbs" can be countered to some degree – by, for example, a tutor emphasising how skills are developed through practice rather than being innate. Chapters 3, 4 and 5 suggest various ways in which less confident students can be helped to appreciate that their communication abilities are much less fixed and limited than they had believed.

Which of these perspectives on student learning have you found helpful? In what ways were they helpful?

How might you put some of these ideas concerning student learning into practice within your own teaching?

REFERENCES

1. Säljö, R. (1979). *Qualitative Differences in Learning as a Function of the Learner's Conception of the Task*. Reports from the Department of Education, University of Göteborg, no. 76.

2. Van Rossum, E.J. and Schenk, S.M. (1984). The relationship between learning conception, study strategy and learning outcome. *British Journal of Educational Psychology*, 54, pp. 73-83.

3. Marton, F. and Säljö, R. (1984). Approaches to learning. In F. Marton, D. Hounsell, N. Entwistle (eds.) *The Experience of Learning*. Edinburgh, Scottish Academic Press.

4. Marton, F. and Säljö, R. (1984) op. cit.

5. Entwistle, N. (1992). *The Impact of Teaching on Learning Outcomes in Higher Education: A Literature Review*. Sheffield: CVCP Universities' Staff Development Unit.

6. Entwistle, N. (1992) op. cit.

7. Anderson, C. (1993a). The purposes and nature of talk in university tutorials in social science subjects. Paper presented at 5th EARLI conference, Aix-en-Provence, 1993

8. Anderson, C. (1993b). University students' perceptions of their experience of tutorial groups. In E. de Graaff and P. A. J. Bouhuijs (eds.) *Implementation of Problem-based Learning in Higher Education*. Amsterdam, Thesis Publishers.

9. Pask, G. (1976). Learning styles and strategies. *British Journal of Educational Psychology*, 46, pp. 4-11.

10. Entwistle, N. (1992) op. cit.

11. Entwistle, N. (1992) op. cit.

12. Anderson, C. (1993b). op. cit.

13. Bandura, A. (1989). Human agency in social cognitive theory. *American Psychologist*, 44, 9, pp. 1175-1184.

14. Entwistle, N. (1988). Motivational factors in students' approaches to learning. In R.R. Schmeck (ed.) *Learning Strategies and Learning Styles*. New York: Plenum.

15. Dweck, C.S. (1986). Motivational processes affecting learning. *American Psychologist*, 41, 10, pp. 1040-1048.

16. Dweck, C.S. (1986) op. cit.

Chapter 9

Working with Others

Fred Forster and Miesbeth Knottenbelt

INTRODUCTION

As part of their everyday work, lecturers, tutors and demonstrators alike are in frequent contact with a wide range of university colleagues on whose knowledge and experience they rely in carrying out their responsibilities effectively.

Figure 1 shows in graphic form the many different colleagues with whom part-time teachers are likely to interact for a variety of purposes. Course leaders and lecturers, for example, are a vital source of information on curriculum and teaching matters. Liaison with library staff is important in clarifying arrangements for access for students to appropriate reading and study materials. And secretaries and technicians are not only a key source of support as far as teaching materials, equipment or facilities are concerned, but can also advise on the practicalities of getting things done and where to go for further assistance – the sort of information which (sometimes embarrassingly) is known to everyone except the newest member of staff and which therefore tends to be taken for granted.

Elsewhere in this handbook – and particularly in chapters 2, *Roles and Responsibilities,* and 7, *Supporting and Advising Students* – we have discussed some of the individuals who can play a pivotal role in this network of contacts. Here we look in more detail at two groups of colleagues who have a particular contribution to make to the development of the part-time teacher's professional expertise: mentors, and other tutors and demonstrators in the same department or faculty.

WORKING WITH A MENTOR

A mentor is usually an experienced senior academic whose function is to offer guidance and support to a less experienced colleague (a mentee or protégé). In the present context, the main aim of mentoring is to assist new tutors or demonstrators in a variety of ways in developing their professional expertise.

Defined in this way, mentoring hardly seems a novel idea. Indeed, many senior academics may be surprised to learn that their long-time habit of taking less experienced staff under their wing is

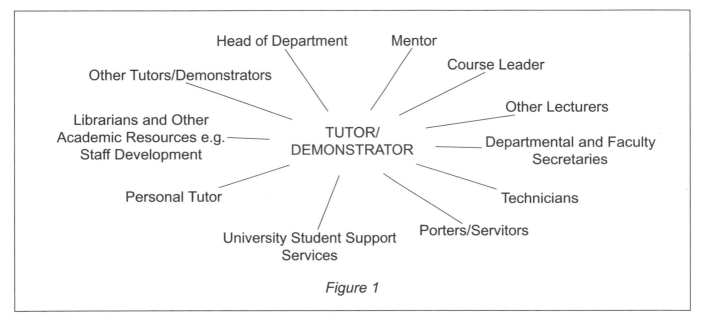

Figure 1

nowadays called 'mentoring'. What distinguishes mentoring in current parlance, however, is that arrangements which were customarily informal – and, it should be said, reliant on the goodwill and commitment of certain colleagues – have become more formalised.

Being part of a mentoring scheme has many potential benefits to offer to new postgraduate and other part-time staff. These benefits include opportunities to:

- become more swiftly acclimatised into the procedures and practices of a department and a faculty;

- gain encouragement from consultation and guidance;

- develop and refine one's professional skills by drawing on the experience and expertise of a mentor;

- talk through and review, at regular intervals, issues and concerns which have arisen during day-to-day work;

- improve one's self confidence with the support and advice of a senior colleague.

Some examples may help to show how mentoring works in practice. During the initial orientation period, for instance, a mentor can help by clarifying the tutor's or demonstrator's specific roles and responsibilities and – just as importantly – advising on where the boundaries to these responsibilities lie, since enthusiastic new staff are more likely to attempt too much than to do too little. The mentor can also help initiate the new colleague into the inner workings of the department, offer briefing on course content and teaching methods, and provide an introduction to other members of the course team.

Once teaching is underway, mentors can help out with queries about marking criteria and assessment practices, monitor the marking of reports and essays, and advise on teaching strategies or techniques for handling problem students. Mentors may also be willing, when invited to do so, to give candid and constructive feedback on their mentee's teaching.

Clearly the potential exists for mentor and mentee to work together fruitfully on a great variety of issues, but there can be a danger of over-burdening the relationship when expectations are unrealistic or demands excessive.

An agreed way of working needs to be established if both parties are to make the most of the relationship. Frank and complete discussions at the outset can go a long way towards getting mentor and mentee off to a strong start, and it is therefore a good idea to use the first meeting to arrive at a clear understanding of purposes and procedures.

If it is to be helpful to you, the initial meeting with your mentor should be an opportunity not just to get to know one another but also to:

- talk through your teaching contract and clarify any uncertainties;

- become acquainted with relevant departmental policies and practices;

- establish guidelines for the mentoring relationship;

- agree when you will next meet and what issues ought to be on the agenda.

A variety of specific issues will also need to be clarified, either at the initial meeting or subsequently, once regular meetings are underway. These issues include:

- how much time is to be set aside for mentoring;

- how often the two of you should meet, and for how long;

- what will be expected of each of you if the mentoring relationship is to work well;

- how confidential matters are best dealt with;

- issues that are off-limits as far as the mentoring relationship is concerned (e.g. personal matters);

- how you can keep in touch outwith your regular meetings;

- how to take stock of how well the mentoring relationship is working, for each of you.

By its very nature, a mentoring relationship will develop and change over time. It is therefore important that the relationship is a two-way professional one, implying the mutual sharing of thoughts and ideas. Too one-sided a relationship, or expectations that are unclear or unrealistic, can lead to disenchantment and even failure.

> *What priorities would you like to address at your first meeting with your mentor (assuming that you have not yet formally met) ?*

CONTACTS WITH OTHER TUTORS AND DEMONSTRATORS

Informal networks of contacts can be just as valuable as formal ones, and meeting other demonstrators and tutors regularly to share experiences can also be a good source of advice and support, for you personally and for them. And a network of contacts becomes especially helpful when someone is working in a department which does not operate a mentoring scheme, or where widely scattered office and teaching accommodation or workload pressures make liaison with other academic staff difficult.

As with all informal support groups, the content and nature of activities will reflect the interests and concerns of those involved. For example, simply having the opportunity to voice anxieties about the amount of written work to be marked by a given date or the adequacy of students' class preparation may be enough to reassure the new staff member that her or his concerns are not unusual and are shared by others. There can also be profit from pooling growing know-how about the workings of the department, the faculty and the wider university. And getting to know other tutors and demonstrators can be a marvellous source of ideas about running tutorials or labs: how to encourage students to prepare more meticulously, for instance, and what advice to give to students on revising for class tests and end-of-year examinations. Lastly, where tutors or demonstrators work in the same department, it may be feasible to share resources such as desk space, course texts and computing and/or laboratory equipment.

How far a new part-time teacher will wish to make use of opportunities to explore insights and concerns with others is nonetheless an individual matter. Some will feel – sometimes justifiably! – that they have sufficient confidence and expertise to get on with the job independently, drawing on the various sources of information and advice outlined elsewhere in the handbook. But there will also be many who welcome the possibility of confiding in others, and relish the prospect of being part of an informal support group.

Many departments have been quick to recognise the benefits of regular contacts with and between new staff. Some take a lead in hosting or helping to convene meetings of new tutors and demonstrators, or in putting them in touch with old hands – those with a year or more's experience and who therefore already know the ropes. Some departments also regularly organise events such as discussion forums or social gatherings where part-time teachers of all kinds can meet with other academic staff.

Integration of part-time staff into the mainstream of academic affairs is sometimes more readily achieved in small rather than large departments. In small departments with few postgraduates, however, opportunities to interact with peers may be correspondingly limited, and looking beyond the department becomes a virtual necessity. Taking part in workshops or seminars is one useful option. These events are often designed to meet the needs of a particular faculty or school and provide opportunities to meet with colleagues from a wide range of academic disciplines.

> *What initial concerns do you feel you would like to share with other demonstrators/tutors?*
>
> *Is there anything you could do to promote contacts with fellow demonstrators/tutors in your department?*

Chapter 10

Feedback on Teaching

Kate Day

INTRODUCTION

Tutors' and demonstrators' reasons for wanting feedback about their teaching practices are usually a mixture of the personal and the professional. Every part-time teacher is likely to be interested to know in a general way how he or she is doing and how things are going, and while some are keen on having details that will help them consolidate good practice or make improvements, others need to be able to document the quality of their teaching skills. Yet whatever the motivation, no one wants to invest more time and effort than is necessary to produce accurate and useful feedback information.

Indicating broadly how to obtain information that gives a reasonably sound and well-balanced picture is not hard. But the issue of what feedback will prove to be really useful is more problematic. This is partly because teaching practices vary widely within as well as across disciplines. There are choices to be made about which aspects of tutorials or practical classes and of the contributions made by part-time teachers (including marking where appropriate) will form the main focus of the feedback. It is also partly because of the different ways in which feedback can be sought. Some methods of feedback are designed to encourage written or verbal comments in a very open-ended way, while others such as questionnaires may restrict the range of answers to a small number of fixed choices.

Tutors and demonstrators therefore need to think through their own feedback requirements, in the light of, for example, their responsibilities, the aims, focus and content of their classes, and the relative merits of a broad overview or more close-grained information. How much time can realistically be invested is a further important consideration: the richer the feedback being sought, the more time-consuming it is likely to be to collect and analyse.

Thus, deciding what to do is not altogether straightforward, and tutors and demonstrators will find it helpful to be aware of the possible options and what is entailed in putting them into practice. Accordingly, the two-fold aim of this chapter is

- to identify sources and methods particularly suited to getting feedback on teaching

- to give some practical pointers for collecting, analysing and making use of feedback data.

SOURCES OF FEEDBACK

Before considering what feedback to collect, it is worth establishing what kinds of feedback information may already be routinely available.

Existing Feedback

Most university courses are evaluated on an annual basis, often through the use of student questionnaires, and a good starting point is to find out what information about classes the course monitoring will produce, with a view to supplementing rather than duplicating it. Since the main purpose of this kind of feedback is to gain an overall impression of the effectiveness of a course, it will probably not throw much light on particular teachers or classes, but it will always provide a framework within which to nest perceptions of each teacher's practice.

Also helpful to tutors and demonstrators are the informal impressions that accumulate during the process of running sessions. There are the unobtrusive indications given by students' attendance patterns, how well prepared they are, their willingness to get involved in the class and to contribute to the tasks in hand. There are also the chance discussions with academic staff, such as the course leader, a lecturer, or supervisor, and with other part-time colleagues on the same or another course. Interlaced with these, and to some extent feeding on them, are one's own feelings and reflections about what has been happening.

Sometimes it is quite safe to rely on these informal impressions, but on other occasions they can turn out to be partial or premature. The result might of course be to give too rosy a view, but more commonly the effects are in the opposite direction because tutors and demonstrators – especially new recruits – are prone to self-criticism and quicker to pick up on the negatives than the positives. One difficult student, whose disaffection may be quite unrelated to the class, can therefore easily attract more attention than many well satisfied fellow students. A particular comment may be misinformed or unrepresentative, and, as tutors and demonstrators will experience if they take more than one group, classes have a dynamic and life of their own, with both their high points and their sticky patches occurring at moments that are not necessarily predictable.

Feedback Generated by a Tutor or Demonstrator

Since existing channels of feedback are seldom sufficient in themselves to meet most teachers' needs, it makes good sense to obtain some additional systematic feedback.

The ideal in evaluation is to use multiple sources and methods for collecting feedback and to do so several times, rather than taking the equivalent of a single snapshot, from a single vantage point on a single occasion. This maximises opportunities for what is usually called 'triangulation': bringing together findings drawn from different perspectives is more likely to reveal the consistencies amongst diverse reactions or pointers for action. In everyday practice, however, this ideal is difficult to achieve. It is a matter of devising a strategy that will serve well enough, balancing some degree of triangulation against the need for economy of effort.

The three main sources of feedback that part-time teachers can tap are themselves, their students and their academic colleagues. Each is equipped to comment better on some aspects than others. Tutors and demonstrators, for instance, can build up their own sense of areas of strength and weakness, since they are the insiders who know what they are aiming to achieve in their practicals and tutorials and how they are constrained by the resources and facilities available. Students, who will have been exposed to several teaching styles, have a vested interest in relaying their impressions and reactions, which may or may not coincide with the tutor's

perceptions. And the watching brief that other teaching colleagues (and particularly mentors) keep on how part-time staff are faring will be informed by the depth of their own subject expertise and teaching experience.

FOCUSING THE FEEDBACK

In explicitly seeking feedback, university teachers can exercise a degree of control over which aspects of their teaching receive critical appraisal. As far as tutoring and demonstrating are concerned, the most valuable comments will generally be about those dimensions for which tutors or demonstrators have major responsibility and some discretion, together with those related to notions of what constitutes effective teaching.

Feedback on Tutorials

Generally speaking tutors have greater discretion than demonstrators over what is dealt with in tutorials and how it is tackled. A list of questions like those given below will therefore be helpful in reviewing possibilities and refining ideas about what feedback will be especially important.

- How well-integrated are the tutorials with other aspects of the course?
- How relevant are the topics addressed in tutorials?
- Is the mix of tutorial activities on offer sufficiently varied?
- Are students given adequate opportunities to participate?
- How appropriate is the amount of preparation required for tutorials?
- How well prepared is the tutor?
- How satisfactory is the tutor's knowledge of the subject-matter?
- How successful is the tutor in facilitating discussion?
- How well does the tutor succeed in stimulating students' interest in the tutorial topics?
- Is sufficient use made of handouts and other teaching aids?
- Are handouts and other teaching aids used effectively?
- How approachable is the tutor?
- Are students given regular feedback on their progress?

- How helpful is the feedback given to students on their written work?

- Overall, how satisfied are students with the tutorials?

If you are a tutor, which of these sorts of issues are likely to be particularly important for you? Are there any that are not applicable? What would you consider adding to the listing?

Feedback on Practicals

Giving careful thought to what kinds of feedback will be most helpful applies equally to practical and laboratory teaching. But since practical classes are usually carefully planned by more senior staff to ensure good integration with lectures, tutorials and course materials, the scope of questions is likely to be correspondingly narrower than for tutorials, e.g.:

- How realistic are the demands made in the practicals on students' grasp of subject-matter covered in the lectures?

- Are connections between practical work and theoretical background readily apparent?

- How satisfactory is the demonstrators' knowledge of the subject matter?

- What steps does the demonstrator take to ensure that practicals run smoothly (e.g. students adequately briefed, equipment and facilities in good working order, adequate time allocated for the activities set)?

- How approachable is the demonstrator?

- How successful is the demonstrator in responding to questions and queries promptly and effectively?

- How well does the demonstrator succeed in stimulating and sustaining students' interest in practical work?

- How effective is the demonstrator in marking practical or laboratory reports, and in giving students feedback on these?

- Overall, how satisfied are students with the conduct of practicals?

If you are a demonstrator, which of these sorts of issues are likely to be particularly important for you? Are there any that are not applicable? What would you consider adding to the listing?

Finally, advantageous though it is for tutors and demonstrators to clarify those issues on which they would most welcome feedback, students and academic colleagues ought to be given some opportunities to comment on the issues which they (rather than simply the tutor or demonstrator) see as most salient. A blend of well-targeted and more open-ended feedback is therefore highly desirable.

FEEDBACK METHODS

In the minds of many undergraduate students and their teachers, feedback is often very firmly linked to the use of questionnaires. In fact, there are many different methods that can be used, although each method is usually associated with a particular source of feedback, whether it be self, students or academic colleagues. *Figure 1* summarises the methods which are reviewed in this section of the chapter.

SOURCES AND METHODS OF FEEDBACK

Feedback from Self
- checklists and pro formas
- logs and diaries

Feedback from Academic Staff
- previewing and reviewing
- scrutiny of teaching materials

Feedback from Students
- structured group discussion
- simple forms of questionnaire

Figure 1

There are some deliberate omissions from this list. Neither direct observation (where a colleague is a sitter-in) nor indirect observation (using a video or audio recording) is considered appropriate to tutors' or demonstrators' needs, since both can be intrusive and disrupt the working atmosphere of a class that is running well.

Similarly, formal interviews have been excluded, since conducting and transcribing them would be too time-consuming in relation to the knowledge gained, some of which at least could be accessed by more economical means.

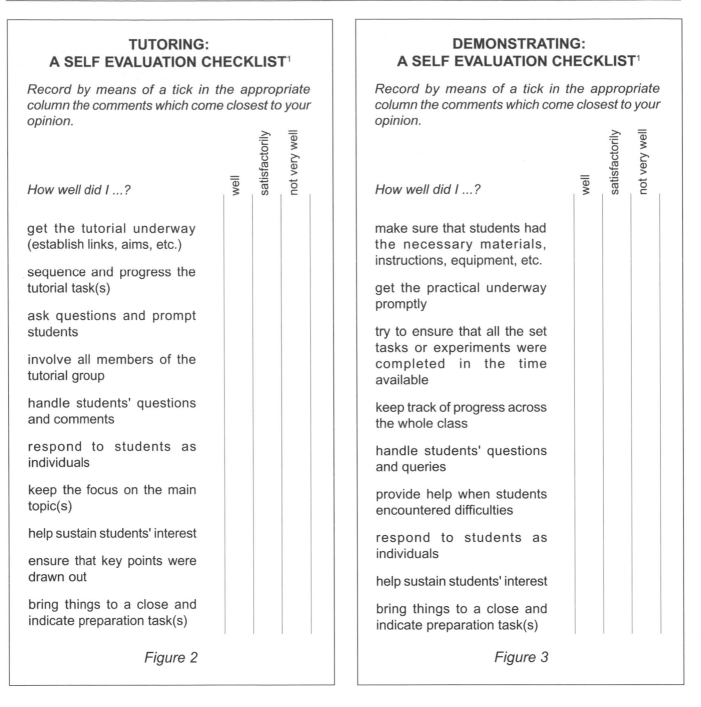

TUTORING:
A SELF EVALUATION CHECKLIST[1]

Record by means of a tick in the appropriate column the comments which come closest to your opinion.

How well did I ...?

— well
— satisfactorily
— not very well

get the tutorial underway (establish links, aims, etc.)

sequence and progress the tutorial task(s)

ask questions and prompt students

involve all members of the tutorial group

handle students' questions and comments

respond to students as individuals

keep the focus on the main topic(s)

help sustain students' interest

ensure that key points were drawn out

bring things to a close and indicate preparation task(s)

Figure 2

DEMONSTRATING:
A SELF EVALUATION CHECKLIST[1]

Record by means of a tick in the appropriate column the comments which come closest to your opinion.

How well did I ...?

— well
— satisfactorily
— not very well

make sure that students had the necessary materials, instructions, equipment, etc.

get the practical underway promptly

try to ensure that all the set tasks or experiments were completed in the time available

keep track of progress across the whole class

handle students' questions and queries

provide help when students encountered difficulties

respond to students as individuals

help sustain students' interest

bring things to a close and indicate preparation task(s)

Figure 3

Feedback from Self

One way of encouraging self-reflection in a productively focused way is to use a checklist such as the examples given in *figures 2* and *3*, which call for a self-rating of performance on a number of key dimensions. If the tutorial or practical concerned is likely to be repeated at some future date, tutors and demonstrators can usefully supplement the completed checklist with snippets of additional background information about what they did or did not do, together with any ideas on what to try next time around.

The pro formas in *figures 4* and *5* are more general but also explicitly forward-looking in their focus, and can be a useful spur to noting down thoughts

generated at the time. Since teaching is fitted in alongside other commitments, it is not surprising that ideas and insights which strike tutors and demonstrators in the course of carrying out their teaching tend to fade unless captured whilst still relatively fresh and clear. Tutors and demonstrators can carry out similar logging functions in lots of different ways, including:

- keeping a regular teaching diary;

- maintaining a loose-leaf collection of reflections, jotted down as and when this seems worthwhile;

- embellishing preparation notes with 'Post-its', recording thoughts and ideas immediately after the class concerned.

None of these options need take up a lot of your time. The important thing is to be able to lay hands on the information when required.

Feedback from Academic Staff

Previewing and reviewing probably call for little explanation: they are techniques for engaging in dialogue, either before or after a tutorial or practical session, with someone who has an informed understanding of the course and its students. Previewing revolves around the question "How well is this likely to work?". The academic colleague's role is to assist you in anticipating and forestalling any problems which might arise in connection with your plans and ideas for a forthcoming class. In reviewing – sometimes called debriefing – you share with your colleague your impression of how the class has gone, whatever its peaks and troughs, and together you explore why as well as what happened in the course of the session, and how you might most benefit from the experience.

Openness, sensitivity, and a supportive attitude on the part of the colleague are the main requirements for previewing and reviewing to work well, and either can be done at any time. The same applies to the scrutiny of tutorial materials or laboratory worksheets, and is another useful feedback activity, whether associated with previewing or reviewing, or undertaken separately.

Needless to say, the existence of a mentoring relationship enlarges the scope for more sustained feedback from and interaction with an experienced academic colleague, and might well benefit from an established pattern of meetings for the regular review of progress.

> *How do you think previewing and reviewing could help you to strengthen your expertise as a teacher? At what points over the coming term or year would previewing or reviewing be most helpful?*

NEXT TIME I GIVE THIS TUTORIAL/PRACTICAL

Topic: Date:

When I gave this tutorial/practical, what seemed to go well was ...

And what didn't seem to go as well as I'd wish was ...

The next time I give this tutorial/practical

I should omit ...

I should change ...

I should add ...

Figure 4

REFLECTIONS ON YOUR TEACHING[2]

As soon as possible after taking a tutorial or practical class, write a short account of what took place. Concentrate on what actually happened, rather than attempting to evaluate it:

Now try to categorise your observations using the following headings:

Planned things I did – before and during the session – which helped students learn.

Anything unplanned I did during the class which seemed to be helpful.

Anything – planned or unplanned – which may have hindered students' learning.

Figure 5

Feedback from Students

Since group discussion is the characteristic tutorial method, the case for tutors deploying the same approach to obtaining feedback from their tutees is a compelling one. But it is a useful approach for demonstrators too, since they also have the advantage of working regularly with a group of students they have come to know well.

As a feedback technique, group discussion has distinctive strengths: it gives opportunities for exploring issues in depth, weighing the significance of points raised and clarifying students' suggestions. If it is to work well, however, it needs a clear framework or structure which will both help to ensure that key issues are addressed and encourage everyone to make contributions of their own.

One possible starting point is to ask your students to identify the main strengths and weaknesses of their tutorials or practical classes, or to suggest what changes they think would be helpful. Another is to provide a working agenda (of the kind illustrated earlier), while at the same time encouraging the group to substitute or add other items as they see fit. It also helps if you appoint one of the students in the group to assist in recording the main discussion points, which can be checked over before a summary note of the findings is produced. Whilst group discussion does take up valuable time in eliciting views, this is counterbalanced by the effort saved in the painstaking analysis which other methods of feedback would necessitate, since students' views are recorded and collated as an integral part of the process. Should you feel that students are likely to be too inhibited by the lack of anonymity to voice their opinions – perhaps for fear of causing embarrassment or of being disadvantaged in some way – one feasible solution might be to involve a trusted third party in running the feedback session.

A refreshingly different way of getting pointers as to how classes are progressing is to give out 'Post-it' slips for students to label with three simple headings, as illustrated in *figure 6*. You then ask the students to write below each heading what they would like you to stop, start and continue doing in tutorials or practicals during the next part of the course. The 'Post-it' notes can be displayed immediately on a board, wall, or the back of a door, and after they have been collected up you can group similar comments together to identify the main themes.

Questionnaires are of course a third option, but a light touch is essential, for two reasons. First, questionnaires may look straightforward, but in reality designing and processing a good questionnaire calls for considerable effort and expertise. Second, feedback questionnaires are in such widespread use that some students are

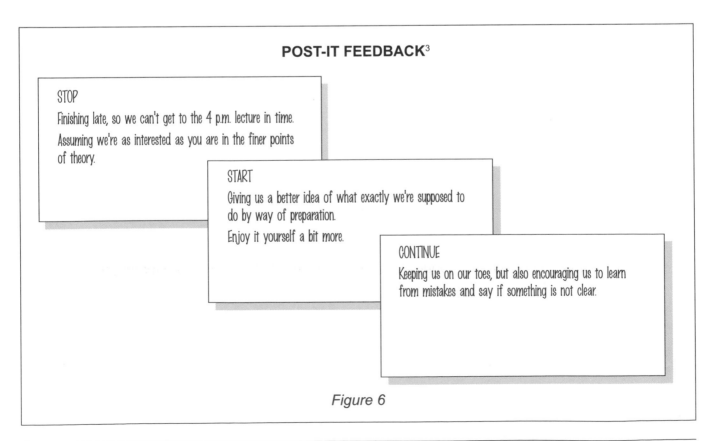

Figure 6

experiencing 'questionnaire-fatigue', and there is a growing reluctance to fill them in with careful thought or attention to detail.

One way of achieving a light touch is to use the one-minute questionnaire. This entails asking students to jot down their answers to one or two questions, which are handed in as they leave. The focus could be related to the substance of the tutorial or practical class:

- 'What is the most significant thing that you learned today?'

- 'What question is uppermost in your mind at the end of this tutorial/practical?'

or it might touch on what the group was like:

- 'How do you feel the class went today?'

- 'What would have made it better for you?'

While students would feel put on the spot if asked directly, their written responses are more likely to give insights into their experiences and what they are taking from them. A similar approach can also be used to get feedback at the end of a course or part-course, asking students to indicate, for example:

- 'Things you found most valuable, and why.'

- 'Things you found least valuable, and why.'

- 'Your ideas for improvements.'

If you feel that more than a light touch is merited

A TUTORIAL QUESTIONNAIRE[4]

Please put a tick in the appropriate box to indicate your response to each of the following statements about the tutorials you attended as part of the course. Thank you very much.

The tutorials	✓✓	✓	?	X	XX
• covered key areas and ideas	☐	☐	☐	☐	☐
• were well linked to lectures	☐	☐	☐	☐	☐
• were well planned and structured	☐	☐	☐	☐	☐
• encouraged students to prepare properly	☐	☐	☐	☐	☐
• were lively and stimulating	☐	☐	☐	☐	☐
The tutor					
• helped students to participate and contribute	☐	☐	☐	☐	☐
• was interested in students and their progress	☐	☐	☐	☐	☐
• acted as an effective group leader	☐	☐	☐	☐	☐
As a student					
• I looked forward to the tutorials	☐	☐	☐	☐	☐
• I enjoyed being in the tutorials	☐	☐	☐	☐	☐
• I learned a lot from the tutorials	☐	☐	☐	☐	☐

Please add below any comments about what would have made the tutorials better for you

✓✓ = strongly agree, ✓ = agree, ? = unsure, X = disagree, XX = strongly disagree

Figure 7

---

and will work with your students, you could consider adapting an off-the-shelf questionnaire of the kind shown in *figures 7* and *8*. Ready-made questionnaires rarely offer an exact match with a teacher's particular requirements, but can of course be modified to suit specific contexts. Your institution's staff development or training unit may well have a collection of feedback questionnaires for you to consult and see the varied range of what has already been developed.

PRACTICAL CONSIDERATIONS

Implicit in this discussion of feedback methods has been the notion that, apart from eliciting information from all three sources, most teachers will also welcome and benefit from feedback of two broad kinds: formative feedback (gathered as the classes are in progress and giving the opportunity to make adjustments or take a fresh approach) and summative feedback (collected as the tutorials or practicals come to an end and giving an overall view of their strengths and weaknesses). So the question of when to obtain feedback – en route or at the finish – cannot easily be viewed in simple either/or terms. At base, it is a matter of striking an appropriate balance between how much feedback would be helpful to you as a part-time teacher and what can be realistically handled in practice. Students and academic staff will certainly be encouraged to give feedback if they feel that it is informing practice, and indeed feedback loses its rationale unless this is the case. On the other hand, no one wants to feel overburdened with supplying or processing

---

A QUESTIONNAIRE ON PRACTICALS[4]

Please put a tick in the appropriate box to indicate your response to each of the following statements about the practicals you attended as part of the course. Thank you very much.

	✓✓	✓	?	X	XX
The practicals					
• covered key areas and ideas	☐	☐	☐	☐	☐
• were well linked to lectures	☐	☐	☐	☐	☐
• helped relate theory to practice	☐	☐	☐	☐	☐
• were well planned and structured	☐	☐	☐	☐	☐
• were lively and stimulating	☐	☐	☐	☐	☐
The demonstrator					
• made clear what was expected of students	☐	☐	☐	☐	☐
• helped students with any difficulties they encountered	☐	☐	☐	☐	☐
• was interested in students and their progress	☐	☐	☐	☐	☐
As a student					
• I looked forward to the practicals	☐	☐	☐	☐	☐
• I enjoyed being in the practicals	☐	☐	☐	☐	☐
• I learned a lot from the practicals	☐	☐	☐	☐	☐

Please add below any comments about what would have made the practicals better for you

✓✓ = strongly agree, ✓ = agree, ? = unsure, X = disagree, XX = strongly disagree

Figure 8

---

feedback, and in no sense should feedback be so intrusive that it gets in the way of the main business of teaching and learning.

Most of the methods described in this chapter, and their use with the relatively small numbers characteristic of tutorial groups or practical classes, mean that data analysis is not the substantial undertaking it can be with extensive questionnaires and very large classes. If some of the feedback is in the form of students' responses to questionnaire items, applying sophisticated statistical procedures is unlikely to be warranted. It is generally sufficient to construct a simple table giving the total number of responses for each item and their percentage equivalents, which rarely requires more than the assistance of a hand-held calculator. The open-ended comments generated by the other methods discussed also need to be analysed systematically. This entails organising comments into relevant categories (e.g. those relating to various aspects of the class content, the tutor's or demonstrator's management of the session, and the learning outcomes) and then, where necessary, identifying key themes which may cut across comment categories. The task is often as easily done manually (e.g. by xeroxing, cutting up and physically sorting the responses into sensible groupings), as on a computer. Whatever form the data takes, your main aim should be to produce an accurate summary of the findings, which can then be considered alongside whatever else has emerged, in arriving at a reasonably rounded and even-handed picture of the classes and the teaching.

The same principle applies in making sense of any item of data. No single piece of evidence should be taken too seriously by itself: more important are the *overall* indications of strengths and weaknesses, together with any pointers for making improvements. Nor should the feedback necessarily be taken too personally; for tutorials and practical classes cannot be isolated from the rest of a course, and the ability to bring about lively, productive sessions is affected by a web of internal and external factors outwith the control of individual tutors or demonstrators, including curriculum content, course structure, assessment

practices, and resources. What will assist the further development of both the part-time teacher and the course is for tutors and demonstrators to discuss with other academic staff, and particularly other experienced members of the course team, what the feedback data might mean and what its practical implications are.

For all tutors and demonstrators, feedback can contribute to what they learn from their teaching experiences. But the other benefits it has will vary, depending on the aspirations of individuals and what the future holds for them. Those who continue to teach in the following year will be much better informed about what action to take in adjusting their teaching approach and building their expertise. Those who are moving on to employment, and not only those on an academic career path, will find it useful to be able to document their skills and achievements as teachers, whilst at the same time displaying the professionalism associated with treating feedback as part and parcel of effective teaching.

REFERENCES

1. Adapted from a self-evaluation checklist for use after a teaching session which has been much reproduced from Gibbs, G., Habeshaw, S. and Habeshaw, T. (1988). *53 Interesting Ways to Appraise Your Teaching*. Bristol: Technical and Educational Services.

2. This is based very much on a checklist which appears in Gibbs, G. (1993). Observing Teaching. SCED Paper 79. Birmingham: Standing Conference on Educational Development.

3. This technique was devised by Phil Race and is very effective in use. See Race, P. and Brown, S. (1993). Getting feedback from your learners. *500 Tips For Tutors*. London: Kogan Page, pp. 66-68.

4. This questionnaire has in fact been specially constructed, drawing on practical experience and ideas from guides to evaluation, such as Ramsden, P. and Dodds, A. (1989). *Improving Teaching and Courses: A Guide to Evaluation*. 2nd edn. Melbourne: University of Melbourne. But it has its origins in a questionnaire for the evaluation of small group teaching produced by the Advisory Centre for University Education at the University of Adelaide. See Roe, E. and McDonald R. (1983). *Informed Professional Judgment: A Guide to Evaluation in Post-Secondary Education*. St Lucia: University of Queensland Press, pp. 180-182.

Chapter 11

Taking Things Forward

Sheila Thompson

INTRODUCTION

This chapter rounds out the preceding chapters by encouraging you to review where you are in your teaching, and then to assess which areas you wish to focus on in further developing your skills. Once you have reviewed your priorities, a realistic way forward may be to work on one or two key areas rather than trying to do everything at once.

The directions in which you will be thinking of developing your teaching expertise will vary. Some tutors and demonstrators may have mastered the 'basics' and feel ready to try out some new strategies, others may just be beginning and need to make sure they get a firm grasp of basic skills.

It is worth bearing in mind that the first-hand experiences you are gaining as a teacher and the skills you are developing, should be useful to your future career path whether or not you choose an academic career. All of the following are valued by employers in many fields:

- group and teamwork skills;

- oral communication skills;

- leadership skills;

- explaining, listening and questioning skills;

- evaluating others;

- reflection on practice.

TAKING STOCK

Before looking at how you can take things forward, it may be helpful to spend a few minutes reviewing where you are now. Whether you are new to tutoring or demonstrating, or already have some experience, this will be an opportunity to take stock of your professional needs, in relation to your teaching responsibilities over the coming year.

If you are just beginning as a part-time teacher, you may want to think about the issues covered in this handbook and pinpoint those which are of most concern to you personally. If you have some experience, you might like to look back and reflect on what skills you have already mastered and what you still need to learn. In either case, why not take a moment or two to review the following?

- What will your teaching responsibilities be over the coming term?

- What will your teaching responsibilities be over the coming year?

- What information will you need to carry out these responsibilities effectively?

- What skills will your responsibilities call for?

- How familiar are you with these skills?

- How can you best ensure that you develop these skills appropriately over the coming weeks?

MOVING FORWARD

To help you make good progress developing these skills as quickly and as effectively as possible, here are some things you may like to try:

- Using this handbook as your key resource. As with all such handbooks, it is likely that you will need to work through it more than once to gain the full benefit.

- Checking that you really do have all the relevant documentation and materials produced by your department and course team. If you have not, then why not make a list of what you do have and check it out, say, with the course leader or your mentor if you have one?

- Familiarising yourself with the main library provision and IT facilities, the departmental library and the administration and secretarial arrangements in your department.

- Finding out about and taking part in training courses and seminars offered to part-time teachers in your institution.

- Thinking about how you can make the most of your mentor and your head of department by raising with them some of your concerns or queries. Their expertise within the department can be particularly valuable to you (see chapter 9, *Working with Others*).

- Finding out about the framework of student support services that exists within the University and how these are linked with the personal tutor system (see chapter 7, *Supporting and Advising Students*.

- Sharing your experiences, ideas, and concerns with other tutors or demonstrators. Those within your department are the obvious ones to work with, but it may also be of benefit to talk to colleagues from other departments (see chapter 9, *Working with Others*). Examples of things you may like to share are:

  - reviewing feedback gathered on your teaching especially using methods like previewing and reviewing (see chapter 10, *Feedback on Tutoring and Demonstrating*)

  - talking about ways you have found for dealing with, for example, silent or over-talkative students

  - looking jointly at some of the written work that has been marked and clarifying ideas about applying assessment criteria (see chapter 6, *Marking and Commenting on Essays* and chapter 4, *Problem-Solving Classes*).

- Keeping records of your work:

  - files of your own materials associated with the course

  - student records of attendance, assignments and formal assessments (it is useful to keep a record of your comments as well as the marks).

- Thinking about what feedback you would find the most helpful, how you are going to collect this feedback and what you are going to do with the information. Chapter 10, *Feedback on Tutoring and Demonstrating*, has lots of ideas for simple and effective ways you can do this. It is not necessarily something you need to do on your own: you could form a group with others on the course.

- Looking at the possibility of keeping a record of your development as a tutor or demonstrator: for example, by keeping a diary or a log, in which you record your thoughts every now and again, on your experiences of leading tutorial or practical groups, or, say, on the kinds of feedback you are giving and how effective you think it is. This is useful as a stocktaking exercise, for recording good ideas and for keeping a record of the skills you are developing.

LOOKING TO THE FUTURE

How much time you will want to and be able to spend on some of these possibilities will depend on a number of factors, one of which will be how you see your own future career development. If, for example, you feel strongly committed to pursuing an academic career, then your part-time teaching will be an important opportunity to acquire some of the basic skills of a university teacher. You may also want to put special effort into developing your expertise, into getting feedback, and into actively exploring sources and resources from chapter 12, *Sources and Resources*.

On the other hand, your long-term career interests may lie elsewhere and an academic career is not going to be your chosen path. You will nevertheless be developing transferable skills that are valued by employers and, like any teacher, you will have the satisfaction of a job well done.

Chapter 12
Sources and Resources
Sheila Thompson

INTRODUCTION

The handbook as a whole offers a grounding in the most important aspects of tutoring and demonstrating. Allied to guidance from within the department, it should enable new part-time staff to get to grips with their roles and responsibilities quickly and effectively. However, there may be a variety of issues that arise in your every day work as a teacher which you wish to pursue further. The aim of this chapter therefore is to outline what additional sources and resources you might draw on. Needless to say, there is no expectation that you will want to take up more than a few of the opportunities offered here, or that you will have the time to do so.

MAIN SOURCES

Four sources of further help are listed which you may find useful:

- colleagues
- organisations which offer guidance and support to students
- workshops, seminars and short courses
- printed guides.

Colleagues

Other colleagues in your department are obviously important resources. They can be of immediate and direct help to you. These colleagues may be lecturing staff, your mentor, a personal tutor, a course leader, other part-time teachers, and also the administrative, secretarial and technical staff of the department. Chapter 9, *Working with Others*, gives details of the ways useful working relationships can be built up with departmental and other colleagues.

Organisations Offering Guidance and Support to Students

Figure 1 lists the agencies that offer help and advice to students and that you will find in most large institutions. It would be helpful for you to keep a contact telephone number or email address for the agencies you consider the most important in your university or college.

Workshops, Seminars and Short Courses

A wide range of staff training and development opportunities are now available in universities and colleges most of which have a staff development or

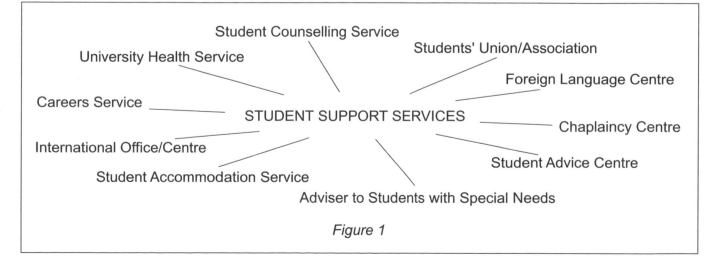

Figure 1

teaching-learning centre through which programmes are organised. There may also be specific training offered to you from within your department, school or faculty. Look out for any of these training opportunities in staff newsletters and on notice-boards.

Printed Guides

Below are details of some key texts that will be of use to you should you wish to find out more about *specific* aspects of tutoring and demonstrating.

General Issues in Teaching

Race, P. and Brown, S. (1993)   *new ed 2005*
500 Tips For Tutors
London: Kogan Page, 130pp, ISBN 0 7494 0987 8

> This is a start-anywhere, dip-in resource suitable both for novices and more experienced tutors. The 500 'ideas' are grouped as general study skills, starting off and working together, lectures and written work, learning resources, assessment, and life skills.

Brown, G. and Atkins, M. (1988)
Effective Teaching in Higher Education
London: Methuen, 245pp, ISBN 0 416 09082 6

> Probably one of the best overall texts on teaching and learning in higher education. Comprehensive coverage is given to lecturing, small group teaching, laboratory teaching, research and project supervision, student learning and helping students to learn. (The chapter on lecturing may be useful if you are asked to lecture.)

Tutoring

Gibbs, G. Habeshaw, S. and Habeshaw, T. (1988)
53 Interesting Things To Do In Your Seminars And Tutorials
(3rd edition) Bristol: Technical and Educational Services Ltd.,136pp, ISBN 0 947885 07 2

> The 53 suggestions are grouped under the headings of: starting off, student-led seminars, group work, encouraging students to participate, encouraging students to take responsibility, evaluating the work of the group, written material, expressing feelings. It is a rich compendium for tutors seeking ways to maximise effective student participation.

Lublin, J. (1987)
Conducting Tutorials
(HERDSA Green Guide No.6) Kensington, New South Wales: Higher Education Research and Development Society of Australasia, 40pp, ISBN 0 908557 08 6

> This booklet begins by reviewing some fundamental issues such as why tutorials are important, what happens in them and the role of the tutor. Subsequently four themes are dealt with: types of tutorial, getting started, strategies and techniques, problems. A reflective review of the major skills needed to conduct tutorials is presented.

Demonstrating

Gibbs, G and Jaques, D (1989)
Labs and Practicals
Oxford: Oxford Centre for Staff Development, Oxford Brooks University, 106pp, ISBN 1 873576 01 3

> This book is easily browsed and covers: aims and objectives, lab guides, contexts, problem solving, co-operative learning, lab technicians, report writing, assessment and giving feedback.

Boud, D Dunn, J and Hegarty-Hazel, E (1986)
Teaching in Laboratories
Society for Research into Higher Education, Milton Keynes, Open University Press, 182pp, ISBN 0 335 15609 6

> This detailed and informative guide covers design and organisation of laboratory activities, teaching strategies, assessment and monitoring of laboratory teaching. Case studies are used to illustrate practice.

Problem Solving Classes

Hubbard, R (1990)
53 Interesting Ways to Teach Mathematics
Bristol, Technical and Educational Services Ltd., 150pp, ISBN 0 9 47885 60 9

> The usual dip-into format of the '53' series, full of practical ideas. Contents include conducting tutorials, using exercises, developing study skills and assessing learning.

Marking and Feedback

Hounsell, D. and Murray, R. (1992)
Essay Writing for Active Learning
(Effective Learning and Teaching in Higher Education, Module 9) Sheffield: Committee of Vice Chancellors and Principals, Universities' Staff Development Unit, 60pp (part 1), 48pp (part 2)

> A very informative guide covering: perspectives on essay writing, why ask students to write essays, what does essay writing entail, facilitating essay writing and feedback. Part 2 includes examples of essay guidance given to students in a variety of disciplines.

Student Learning

Entwistle, N. (1992)
The Impact of Teaching on Learning Outcomes in Higher Education: A Literature Review
Sheffield: Committee of Vice Chancellors and Principals, Universities' Staff Development Unit, 59pp

> An up-to-date and comprehensive review of the literature relating to student learning in higher education.

Study Skills and Transferable Skills

Of interest to you:

Habeshaw, T., Gibbs, G. and Habeshaw, S. (1989)
53 Interesting Ways Of Helping Your Students To Study
(2nd edition) Bristol: Technical and Educational Services Ltd., 200pp, ISBN 0 947885 16 1

> A book to dip into, with each of the 53 ideas standing alone. It covers organising study, reading and note-taking, writing, learning with others, revising and exams. The focus throughout is on how to help students achieve proficiency in these skills.

Kemp, R. and Race, P. (1992)
Promoting the Development of Personal and Professional Skills
(Effective Learning and Teaching in Higher Education, Module 10) Sheffield: Committee of Vice Chancellors and Principals, Universities' Staff Development Unit, 84pp (part 1), 68pp (part 2)

> This publication includes sections on how to help develop students' communication skills, students' team skills, and students' problem solving skills. There are examples given alongside the basic principles and there are detailed case studies in part 2.

For your students:

Race, P. (1992)
500 Tips for Students
Oxford: Blackwell, 148pp, ISBN 0 631 18851 7

> Simple, practical hints for students from starting out to finding your feet. It covers such topics as: essay writing, giving seminars, problem solving, exams. and time management. The emphasis is on active learning, and on helping students take increased responsibility for their own learning.

Marshall, L. and Rowland, F. (1993)
A Guide to Learning Independently
(2nd edition) Buckingham: Open University Press, 254pp, ISBN 0 335 19171 1

> An excellent general study guide offering a range of ideas and techniques to choose from based on the approach that there is no one way of learning. It covers organising study, using libraries, reading, lectures, tutorials, and writing.

Northedge, A. (1990)
The Good Study Guide
Milton Keynes: Open University, 248pp, ISBN 0 7492 0044 8

> A good general study guide to help refine study technique. It includes examples throughout and exercises to practice techniques. It covers organising yourself, reading and note-taking, lectures, groupwork, writing essays and exams.

Clanchy, J. and Ballard, B. (1992)
How to Write Essays: A Practical Guide for Students
(new edition) Melbourne: Longman Cheshire, 152pp, ISBN 0 582 87497 1

> An invaluable book on essay writing for any discipline. Its practical approach focuses on analysing a topic, reading and research, note-taking, planning and drafting, editing, and exam essays. The appendices provide materials for practising techniques.

Taylor, G. (1989)
The Student's Writing Guide for the Arts and Social Sciences
Cambridge: Cambridge University Press, 250pp, ISBN 0 521 36905 3

> This book will assist students with the problems they may face in academic writing. Topics covered are reading, note-taking, interpretation and analysis, structuring an essay, and use of language. Examples of students' essays are used throughout.

Feedback

O'Neil, M. & Pennington, G. (1992)

Evaluating Teaching and Courses from an Active Learning Perspective

(Effective Learning and Teaching in Higher Education, Module 12) Sheffield: Committee of Vice Chancellors and Principals, Universities' Staff Development Unit, 72pp (part 1), 64pp (part 2)

> Part 1 includes techniques for evaluating teaching using students, self and peers. There are sections on developing portfolios and on reviewing courses. Misconceptions about evaluations of teaching are also included. Part 2 has examples of evaluation frameworks and reports of evaluations in action across different disciplines.

Index